ARCHAEOLOGY

LIFE IN THE TRENCHES

It Ain't All Golden Masks and
Crystal Skulls

Nick Adams

CONTENTS

ACKNOWLEDGEMENTS

During almost fifty years of living and breathing archaeology, a lot of people have helped along the way, some of whom are mentioned in the text and some are not. If you're reading this and don't find your name here, please don't be insulted or upset – just know that your contribution is valued, if temporarily overlooked.

So, in no particular order, thanks to: Trev England, John Clipson, Steve Dunmore, Andrew Rogerson, Julia Rogerson, Julie Jones, Andrew Jones, Andrew Lawson, Marie Dewhirst, Don MacLeod, Beverlee Ritchie, Bill Fox, Bill Ross, Grace, Jay and Barb Rajnovich, Thor and Julie Conway, Dan Strom, Bruce Stewart, Sue Bazely, Neal Ferris, Dean Jacobs, Jim Sherratt, Dana Poulton, Christine Dodd, Laurie Jackson, Chris Andersen, Paul Racher, Phil Woodley, Ron Williamson, Nick Gromoff, Hugh Daechsel, Brenda Kennett, Jeff Earl, Rob von Bitter, Paige Cambell, Gary Brewer, Jerry O'Reilly, Rick Hornsby, Scott Milne, Ray Bonenberg, John Hornsby, Mark Purchase and a host of clients, engineers, planners and contacts who have worked to keep me busy.

Over the years many people have worked with me and some have even been daft enough to keep at it for decades. Their work, dedication, conversation and insights have been, and continue to be wonderful, even if we've all heard one another's stories many times over. In particular, my sincere and fondest thanks are due to Steve and John Errington, Chris and Wendy Cadue, Doug Kirk, Peter Cassidy, Phil Whitfield, Sam Adams and Alex Adams. Over the years, they have been the core of my crew, aided and abetted by many others.

Ever since we first met in Sault Ste. Marie, Chris has been canoeing partner, wife, mother of Sam, Emily and Alex, historical researcher, conscience and guide. She has put up with me being away much of the time and has written all the most interesting parts of my reports, for which I have absorbed all the credit.

Special thanks to Betty Andrews for editing the text and purging it of a million unnecessary commas. Oh yes – and for being a great Mother-in-Law.

And of course, the dogs: Mishi, Jenny and Casey, German Shepherds all. Constant companions, who kept us safe from many a squirrel and chipmunk while we worked.

PREFACE

I have met countless people who have said,

"I always wanted to be an archaeologist, but…………..",
followed by some justification as to why they didn't – usually citing lack of job prospects or pressure from parents to 'get a real job'.

Archaeology is a beguiling occupation; who wouldn't be attracted to finding cool, old stuff buried in the ground? It appeals to the child in us all from that first moment we find an abandoned and forgotten toy in the depths of the backyard sand box, while avoiding the cat poop.

I never set out to be an archaeologist (some might argue I'm still not), and yet, almost 50 years after I picked up a shovel on my first dig, I'm still making a living at it. I don't have a felt hat or whip, I'm not a brilliant academic, I don't have a host of books and scholarly publications to my name or tenure or a title. I'm not an expert in anything. To steal a line from my friend Paul, nobody ever says,

"Nick's the guy to ask about that".

The reality is that for every well-known, high-profile archaeologist - the kind you might see doing exciting things on TV - there are legions of lesser characters working in the background. Their work may not be quite as sexy or result in paradigm-changing discoveries, but it is important and valuable.

These are the people who quietly check for archaeological sites on development properties before those nice farm fields get plastered with yet another vinyl and fake brick subdivision. These are the folks who conduct archaeological surveys in remote areas before another priceless river gets dammed (or is that damned?), another vast area gets clear cut or a new road attracts hoards of slovenly tourists to a previously pristine wilderness.

It isn't sexy, but it is essential. With our huge machines and Doozer[1] mentality, our culture is changing the landscape forever, in the process wiping away any traces left by the people who lived here thousands of years before.

---

1   *Characters from 'Fraggle Rock' (a spin-off from the Muppets) who compulsively build things and dress in hard hats, boots etc.*

I didn't start out with the intention that this book would be autobiographical, but as soon as you start describing things you've done in roughly chronological order, it almost inevitably ends up that way. The point is, there are lots of people like me out there, doing archaeological work. Their activities and achievements may not make the news very often, but the cumulative affect of their work is that slowly and surely, our understanding of the past is increasing.

The following chapters are snap-shots of archaeological work. Rather than spending too much time on the scientific and technical, I've tried to convey what an archaeologist's working life is like - well, what this archaeologist's working life has been like, anyway.

CHAPTER 1

EARLY DAYS - UK

Trev England, history teacher, Harold Malley Grammar School 1967:

"Is anyone interested in visiting archaeological excavations at a Roman site near Leamington on Saturday?"

The usual group put up their hands: Mick, Mike, John, Chris and me. We were used to Trev's trips. Those that could get there on their own would do so; everyone else would ride in Trev's car. It would be a sandwiches and muddy boots day.

Trev's trips were a spin-off from sanctioned school trips to places of cultural interest. Our whole class would pile on a bus with a couple of teachers to go somewhere like Hereford or Cirencester to tour the Cathedral, Roman ruins or whatever was the mind-broadening focus of the day. The Cirencester trip has stuck in my mind the best, not because of the amphitheatre or the old walls but because at lunchtime, one of the teachers said,

"We're going into this pub" (pointing to one across the road).

"Be back at the bus at 1:30. We don't expect to see or hear from you until then."

As far as we were concerned, that was licence to go and find a pub of our own. We were all under age, of course, but we had discovered that as long as we broke up into small groups and were quiet and respectful, the pub owners would overlook our youth and serve us.

Trev could be quite a disciplinarian in the classroom but

outside school he was easy going and friendly. Our little group were the keeners; those for whom history wasn't just something to be endured, and he was happy to arrange these little excursions as unofficial extensions of the curriculum.

In these suspicious days, taking a bunch of boys on an unsanctioned trip would never be allowed. We didn't give it a second thought - nor was there ever any reason to.

The site near Leamington was a Roman settlement that had developed near the Fosse Way - a major Roman arterial road between Exeter and Lincoln. We arrived on site and were immediately put to work moving earth by wheel-barrow out of a large, linear trench on the north side of the settlement. I can only assume it was an area where there was no chance of us doing any harm.

From the ground's surface, there was nothing to distinguish the area being excavated from the surrounding fields. There were no building remains and no lumps and bumps to show why they had chosen that place to start digging.

By the time we broke for lunch we had found some pottery, iron nails and a few coins, but nothing to spark the enthusiasm of an impatient sixteen year old. Over near the road, the archaeologists had erected a scaffolding photography tower so I asked the director if I could climb up and take a look. It was disturbingly high and a little bit shaky but eventually I reached the platform at the top.

Looking out to the north, I could see Leamington in the distance, the main area under excavation almost directly below, the office and storage sheds, the piles of back dirt and the trench we had been working in extending down a slight dip to the north. When I turned around though, everything changed. It was one of those rare moments when the world as I knew it suddenly acquired a new dimension.

For as far as I could see, the south side of the Fosse Way was all farm fields of mature wheat gently rippling in the breeze. During the previous night a heavy rain storm had blown some of the crop flat, although most of it was still standing. The rain and wind had been very selective. The flattened areas were all straight lines and rectangles.

Suddenly it clicked. I could see the layout of the whole Roman settlement, neatly defined by the blown down crop. I could see roads, buildings and plazas. In some areas, where walls, roads or heavily compacted ground prevented the roots of the wheat from fully penetrating, the plants above had been more susceptible to the storm and had been blown flat. In others, where the soil was deep and fertile - presumably over ditches, wells, privys and garbage pits - the crop was lush and tall.

When I clambered down, I described what I had seen to the excavation director. He explained that we were working on only a small part of the Chesterton Roman settlement, most of which was indeed on the other side of the Fosse Way. He hadn't noticed the crop blow-down and was soon up the photographic tower with his camera.

Over the next few months I ended up going to help on local excavations regardless of whether anyone else was going. That first experience had opened my eyes and I could now visualize what might be happening in the ground beneath our feet. One Saturdays I might be excavating against the town wall in Warwick; another cleaning off Monastic refectory walls near Redditch. Mostly though, I helped by pushing loaded wheel-barrows up ramps and shovelling dirt from one place to the next. I got to be really good at that.

Southampton

As is so often the case during one's teenage years, eventually archaeology faded into the background as other interests (girls, motorbikes, drinking - sometimes all at once) came to the fore. It wasn't until I decided that being an outdoor education teacher wasn't really the life I wanted, that archaeology entered the picture again.

My old school friend John was working on a dig in Southampton. With a bit of time on my hands and my Panther motorbike at my disposal, I rode south intending to just visit for a day or two. John was working as part of a large crew, excavating a series of Middle Saxon sites within the old town of *Hamwic*, which is now within the industrial heart of the city.

After an evening of socializing, I'd gone to visit the excavations, intending to take off for a ride through the New Forest, but, well, there was soil to move and an impressively steep spiral wheel-barrow ramp to negotiate. Before I'd really thought about it, I'd parked the bike and mucked in. By the end of the day I was on the payroll.

Fieldwork grunts were notoriously poorly-paid at that time. We were called 'volunteers', I suspect so that wages could be artificially low. Nevertheless, housing (of a sort) was provided, and enough money to cover some basic food and the occasional pint.

The house we occupied was on Bugle Street, just up the road from the docks in a rather dingy part of town. The house was city-owned and had been loaned to the archaeological project as a way of keeping it from being vandalized before the whole area was redeveloped. It was certainly rough, but it had a working gas cooking stove, a bunch of bedrooms and some basic furnishings.

The occupants at Bugle Street were constantly changing. At that time, there were so many archaeological projects going on all around the country, that there was a sort of 'hippy trail' of peripatetic field workers who shuffled from one project to the next. Anyone who had stuck around Southampton for more than a couple of months was a fixture.

One fixture was Pat or Paddy - I was never quite sure. He was a monosyllabic Irishman and our main source of consciousness - altering substances. Most of the time, I was far more interested in heading down to the pub for a pint, but on one memorable occasion, after a fairly vigorous drinking session, Pat brewed me some hash tea (since I don't smoke, and never have). I can't remember it having much of an effect, except I gradually became absurdly, ravenously hungry.

At that time of night the only place open was the pub almost next door, which I'd been advised to stay well away from. It was the most notorious dockyard gay bar in the city. It didn't matter. I had to get some crisps or something - anything - to satisfy my urge to eat.

Without being too swell-headed I think it's fair to say I was a good looking boy - or at least, unlike many English lads, most of my features were arranged around my face in some semblance of order - so it wasn't really too surprising that my arrival at the bar caused some interest among the patrons. I'd spent enough time fending off polite but interested gentlemen while hitch-hiking to know the score. I was acutely aware that I had become the focus of attention. If there had been any music playing, it would have suddenly stopped - just like in the movies. Through the alcohol and drug-induced haze I managed to communicate my need to the barman and retreat with my crisps before the situation became too interesting.

The other fixture in Southampton was an attractive young blonde-haired girl. Let's call her Sharon. Sharon didn't live in Bugle Street so I only saw her during the day. Most of the time she was a hard-working, pleasant and competent digger, but she did have one rather unusual and memorable trait.

The site we were working on lay immediately adjacent to the railway line leading to the dock from which passenger ships departed. From time to time, trains full of people would slowly make their way past the site, and since an archaeological excavation in progress was slightly more interesting than gasometers and industrial warehouses, we would see plenty of faces peering eagerly out of the windows. Sharon couldn't be bothered to walk down the road to use the portable toilet at the other archaeological site. She seemed to delight in climbing up on to the railway embankment, pulling down her knickers and squatting to have a pee, just as the train was passing by.

More, I suspect, because of the constantly changing personnel than because of any talent on my part, I soon graduated from being a soil-moving heavy to doing some of the basic recording and surveying and, eventually, to acting as site supervisor for some of the lesser excavation areas. Unlike today, when it seems that an MA is the entry level qualification for wiping your nose, in the archaeology of the early seventies, anyone that showed the slightest aptitude or interest could suddenly find themselves with a considerable amount of responsibility. I was out of my depth, but far too conceited and flattered to admit it.

With people passing through Southampton and only staying for a short time, one tended to hear of projects in other parts of the country on a regular basis. Some of these sounded like archaeological Shangri la, where the pay was good, the archaeology was interesting and the workers were skilled and uninhibited.

Two of the people I'd got to know in Bugle Street were heading to another project, just as I was tiring of Southampton. I'm not going to use their real names - let's call them Jack and Jill -, as Jack subsequently had a stratospheric rise in the British civil service and became rather important.

Jack and Jill were a couple. This was a bit inconvenient for me, since, like just about every male who met Jill, I'd developed a bit of a crush. In a world of rather mousy English girls, Jill was impossibly exotic, with long, straight black hair, high cheek bones and the kind of slim body that makes young men.......well, let's just say she was a bit of a knock-out. Jack was fairly handsome too, but while I found him good company, for some reason, I didn't find him anywhere near as interesting as Jill. They were on their way to work with a friend of theirs who was running an excavation on a Franciscan Friary in Grantham. I was sorry to see them go.

Grantham

I lasted about another week in Southampton. At the time I thought that the stress of being over-worked and under-skilled had got to me, but in retrospect, I think I was on a Quixotic quest to wrestle Jill from Jack's arms.

My motorbike had been left at my mother's house during one of my many visits home, so I packed my gear and hitch-hiked north. I didn't have a clue where the excavation was taking place but as I walked towards Grantham town centre I met a policeman who pointed me in the general direction.

Once I found the excavation, I introduced myself to Andrew, the director, and before long was pushing wheel-barrows again. It turned out that Jack and Jill had only stayed in Grantham long enough to say hello, and had moved on to Suffolk to another project altogether, but there were new people and some interesting holes in the ground so I stayed.

The core staff of the Grantham dig were staying in a pub in the town centre, but Andrew said that since all the rooms were full I could sleep in the dig office trailer until they sorted something out. It didn't take me long to get settled in amid the boxes of artifacts, drawing tables and shovels once everyone was gone for the day. I laid my sleeping bag in the corner and was just in the process of boiling myself some of Pat's special tea when there was an abrupt knock on the door, it swung open, and there was the same policeman I'd met earlier.

"I see you found the place then. Is everything OK?"

I explained that I'd been hired, told him about the pub being full, then - and God knows what I was thinking - offered him a cup of tea. I can only assume he thought it was some fragrant herbal-hippy stuff because mercifully, he declined and soon left me to my luxurious accommodation.

The weeks I spent in Grantham passed in a bit of a blur. Frankly, the only real detail I can remember about my time there was getting a bollocking from Andrew. It was raining too hard to work outside, so we diggers were catching up with some artifact cleaning in the office trailer. I was deep in conversation and distractedly trying to scrub some surface crud off a piece of glass when Andrew noticed that it wasn't crud at all. I was doing my best to remove the decoration from a piece of medieval stained glass.

Eventually the excavations at Grantham were complete and everyone went their separate ways. Many of the people were heading with Andrew to Norfolk to a mysterious place named 'Spong', while I decided it was time to hitch-hike up to Scotland to see if I could see gannets along the coastal waters.

During the time in Grantham I had made friends with an American girl called Julie. There was no romantic interest - indeed, I think she might have been involved with Andrew at the time - but we got along well and decided to stay in touch.

Weeks later, as I was back at my mother's house after a stint of working as a barman and waiter in a hotel on the Isle of Arran and getting my fill of seabirds, I got a letter from Julie. There was a bit of news about the people I knew, and an invitation to turn up at a party in Norfolk to be held the following weekend.

Spong farm is an undistinguished, two storey Norfolk brick and pantile farmhouse a couple of miles south of North Elmham. For the last few years it's been the home of 'Spong Motors' – a car repair place - but in those days it was rented out to archaeologists working at the famous Saxon cemetery on the hill across the road. When I arrived there in mid-afternoon there were already plenty of people, and the barrel of Greene King Abbot which Andrew had acquired through a friend was open and flowing. At some point during the evening before we both got too impaired to remember, Andrew asked me if I'd like to work on a Roman dig he would shortly be starting in south Norfolk. The answer was yes.

Scole

Scole is a small village where the old Roman Road between Venta Icenorum (the predecessor of Norwich) and Londinium (which you can probably figure out for yourselves) crosses the Waveney River. It was well known to those interested in Romano-British studies that a settlement lay buried in the area, as numerous Roman finds had been dug up in gardens and ditches around the village over the years. The area we would be excavating lay just on the north side of the river and was scheduled to become a small housing estate.

Andrew had arranged for us to stay in the empty, former Depwade workhouse/old folks home at Pulham Market. It was a massive brick place with an almost infinite number of rooms, an industrial scale kitchen and various baths complete with hoists and winches. If it was a bit stark and forbidding I don't think we noticed. We were either too tired from long days at the site, too impaired from excessive drinking or too busy racing around the halls in some of the wheelchairs which had been left behind.

Once digging at the site was under way my days tended to follow the same pattern. I would get up early, cycle the six miles to the site then wander around making sure that my notes were up-to-date and that my part of the site recording was in hand before everyone else arrived by car. The crew was relatively small. Other-Andrew, now a rather well-known figure in British archaeology, was our environmentalist, in charge of anything organic. Bruce was tasked with doing all the detailed site plans and photography. Julie, my American friend, recorded all the profiles and sections. Andrew's sister Rose, art student Julia and a couple of others looked after the finds and I was site supervisor. This meant I had the thankless task of making sure that each soil layer, feature, group of artifacts - basically any observable phenomenon to which a number could be attached - got a number, and its relationship to all the things around it was fully recorded. I was also supposed to provide digging guidance to various people who turned up to volunteer to dig for a day or two, and label all the artifact bags with the right numbers. Once again, at times I felt completely at sea, although Andrew was usually around to bail me out.

Our working day started around 8AM and, other than a short break for lunch, during which we fought a running battle with hoards of wasps who would try to nibble our sandwiches and swim in our drinks, would continue uninterrupted until 6PM.

6PM was when the Scole Inn opened. At the end of each working day we usually headed for the bar. Our drinking and relaxation was frequently disturbed by a budgie with an advanced self-abuse issue. At some point during the evening a couple of people would drive back to the workhouse to prepare supper while the rest of us continued relaxing. Once the meal was ready the pub phone would ring and we would head back to base. It was a perfect arrangement.

Although I had worked briefly on a Roman site before, I was unprepared for the complexity of Scole and the sheer abundance of artifacts. Not only was the site stratified (ultimately 4 main phases of occupation spanning the 1st and 3rd centuries A.D. were defined), but there were cess pits, roads, wells, layers of occupation debris, building platforms, postholes and other miscellaneous features cutting through, or sealed by other deposits.

At the end of each day, the back of Andrew's hatchback was filled with artifact bags. By the end of the project, we had excavated almost 700 kilograms of locally-made domestic pottery (coarseware and mortaria) and countless pieces of finer moulded 'Samian Ware' from France and the Rhineland.

It had been a real eye-opener to find 11 Roman coins while we were removing the topsoil by machine. This number jumped to 46 by the end of the excavation. There were copper alloy brooches, corn grinding quern stones, decorated bone and copper alloy pins and iron hardware of various kinds including sheep shears and horse bits - just about everything you can imagine being in use in a small, busy roadside village.

The discovery of the two wells was probably the high point of the excavation. At first we had recognized that a large, dark, roughly-circular soil stain was probably a large pit. We had already encountered a number of cess pits (pits below toilets) in other parts of the site. These pits were always full of interesting artifacts because things dropped in them when they were active were rarely retrieved (think about it!), and, once they went out of use, they were natural places for garbage disposal, so they tended to be full of large items which hadn't been kicking around on the surface long enough to get broken into fragments. I always enjoyed digging in the cess pits. The composition of the lower layers didn't leave one in any doubt as to their primary function: the greasy, yellowish-green clay had a distinctive feel and a very slight residual odour.

As we excavated deeper into the pit, we realized that what we had originally thought was the edge was, in fact, merely a fill layer in an even larger feature. We were only taking out half of the fill at this point, leaving the unexcavated half standing so that we could record the cross section.

Once we found the full breadth of the feature we continued to excavate downwards, recording each layer and fill deposit as we went, bagging the many artifacts according to the layer from which they came.

At about 1.5 metres below the ground surface we started to notice a distinct soil layer present in the middle of the feature and that this was surrounded by a rectangular brown stain. Andrew was called over. He immediately recognized that the brown stain was actually decayed timber, the cribbing of a well.

Excavating the well was a mucky and time-consuming job. The person at the bottom filled buckets of sloppy soil then passed them overhead to someone who then passed them to a third person at ground level. Eventually, soaking wet and covered in muck, we were able to expose the original, and extremely well-preserved oak cribbing which formed the central shaft of the well. The timbers were amazingly solid and were still doing their job - even after 1800 years.

The lower levels within the well were completely wet, but this was an archaeological bonanza. Everything organic, which had ever fallen or had been thrown down the well shaft, was still there: leather shoes, bits of turned wooden furniture, wooden writing tablets, animal bones showing signs of butchering, oyster shells and seeds of wheat, barley and oats as well as all the normal, inorganic refuse one might expect, including brooches, pins and large chunks of pottery.

Later on in the excavation we found a second well; equally deep, with equally well-preserved timbers and abundant artifacts.

Now I look back on it, the thing that amazes me most was that we were all so young yet had such responsibility. I was 22. Andrew, charged with the responsibility for directing the site, managing the money, organizing digging equipment, pumps and permissions and writing the whole thing up to professional standards afterwards, was 24.

Excavation is the sexy side of archaeology, but in practice it's really only a relatively small part of the process. All those finds have to be cleaned using techniques appropriate to the materials. If you try scrubbing delicate bone or copper alloy objects with the same vigour that you might use on tough, Romano-British wheel-thrown pottery, you'll probably end up with some pulp or some gooey green guck in your hands. Some artifacts have to be sent for special conservation treatment. The shoes from the Scole wells, for instance, needed to be stabilized, then permanently stored in conditions where they wouldn't grow a healthy coating of fungus. Everything has to be labelled with a catalogue number which includes information about exactly which soil layer or feature it came from, otherwise, as soon as it is put down in the wrong place on a table (as inevitably happens), most of its archaeological value is lost forever.

Somehow Andrew wangled some money for me to stay on after the excavation and help processing the artifacts. These were early days for the Norfolk Archaeological Unit which gradually became an arm of the Norfolk County Council. The unit was given space in yet another former workhouse – this time in Gressenhall – just a couple of miles down the road from Spong Farm.

My main job that winter was washing and labelling bag after bag of pottery so that a specialist could come and make sense of it all. It was tedious work, but I didn't really mind, and living in Spong farm with people coming and going all the time was highly enjoyable.

At some point Andrew must have asked me if I could draw, as someone was needed to produce the publication drawings based on

Bruce's excellent field drawings and to illustrate the various artifacts we had found. I gave it a go. After a few false starts, a lot of looking at publication drawings in books and journals, and plenty of practice, I was gradually able to produce results, acceptable enough that I remained employed all winter.

Great Yarmouth

After months spent crouched over a drawing table I needed a break. Even though I was cycling to work, swimming at lunchtime and often running in the evenings, I was feeling desk-bound. I had managed to save a little money so I took off for Spain and Morocco for a few weeks on my bicycle.

I returned with a fit body and a sore head from far too many days of indulgence in Fez. I was happy to hear that the Norfolk Unit had another large project in the works in Great Yarmouth, that Andrew would once again be director and the same group of people would be on staff.

Great Yarmouth was a place I knew fairly well. I had been born in our house in Lichfield Road on the south side of the river, and had spent the first 10 years of my life living within range of the bells of St. Nicholas's Church, after which I was named. I was a difficult delivery. I think naming me after the church's saint was my mother's way of saying Thank God that's over'.

From a very early age I was allowed to wander wherever I fancied. I sometimes accompanied the milk-man on his rounds, sitting on, or hanging off the back of his electric milk float. I wandered through Jewson's wood-yard down by the river and stole long strips of wood which we used to spear jellyfish as they drifted past on the tide. We played in the local park where my brother, eager to try out his new Judo skills, threw me on to a broken bottle. I still have the scar on the side of my hand.

There was never any thought about molesters or injury. These were the post-war years. Adults were still reeling from the real dangers they had weathered in the war, and food rationing was still in effect.

In January 1953, 8 feet of water flooded our house as a combination of high tides and stiff on-shore winds breached the sea defences. My first memory is of my father carrying me upstairs as the water rushed into the house. He had our budgerigar in its cage in the other hand. The salty, sewage-laden water virtually destroyed the downstairs. The floors, the joists and even the plaster all had to be replaced once the waters subsided. It's hardly surprising that they had no time for imagined fears; they had experienced enough real ones.

I can only remember having my range limited once. My father had said that we were not allowed to play on the breakwater as the possibility of getting swept into the North Sea was far too great. When he found out that my brothers and I had been hunting crabs there, we were called in for punishment. Being the youngest I was last and he took it easy on me but, like an idiot, I laughed and said 'That didn't hurt'. I was called back for a second helping. I didn't laugh that time.

The archaeological project was on part of Fuller's Hill – the highest part of Great Yarmouth in an area assumed to have been its early core. Yarmouth is built on a narrow sand spit where the River Yare swings parallel to the shore before entering the North Sea. The sand spit seems to be of relatively recent origin. Unlike so many British towns which have ancient roots, Yarmouth does not appear to have been occupied much before the tenth century.

One of the unique characteristics of the town is a series of extremely narrow 'rows' or small lanes, which cross the town between the river and the sea within the area contained within the town wall. Depending on what you read, there are either 145 or 157 of them, each so narrow that special 'troll-carts' were developed to transport goods along them. Although they acquired official numbers in 1804, each used to have a name, including: Kittywitches, Split Gutter, Body Snatchers and (along with many other medieval towns) Gropecuntlane.

As a kid, these narrow alleys with buildings hemming them in along most of their length, were intimidating to me. One day when I was about 6 my brother Tim and I were walking down one of the rows when we passed an open area - a leftover from German bombing during WW2. Suddenly we were surrounded by a group of tough looking kids who were intent on giving us a hard time. I was a bit too young to be much sport but they grabbed Tim and started pushing him around. I panicked, and, crying, fled down the row to the main road where I was eventually able to convince an adult that my brother was being hurt.

By the time we got back it was all smiles. Tim was one of those kids who would never back down from a fight no matter how badly the odds were stacked against him. After a few punches had been thrown the other kids had recognized that there was no way to intimidate him and had decided to be friends. I was still weeping and shaky. Tim was walking a little taller that day.

The excavations were in an area that had been part of Lacon's Brewery. Some of the brewery buildings had been demolished and their footings removed leaving large areas where the underlying ground had been disturbed. Nevertheless, we were able to define an area where damage was minimal and excavation had the possibility of being fruitful. As usual, Andrew had found some accommodation for us in an unoccupied building.

As excavation proceeded we encountered layers of black, greasy sand which were the remains of burned out fishermen's shacks, alternating with thick bands of clean and sterile wind-blown sand. This sand was our biggest problem. It had very little cohesion. If we dug too deeply the sides of the excavation would collapse, covering whatever we had just exposed.

We didn't have the budget to rent the kind of metal cribbing which would have allowed us to excavate straight down. Instead, we had to dig in a series of spits, then cut the surrounding deposits back at a 45 degree angle. Sadly, this meant that the area available for detailed investigation got smaller and smaller the deeper we went.

Although the excavation area we could examine was smaller than we had hoped, it proved to be archaeologically rich and exciting. As each of the fishermen's shacks had burned they had been abandoned, then covered by the wind-blown sand. Everything that had been in or around the shack was still intact, including all the organic refuse, the remains of the fish they had been eating or processing on site.

Other-Andrew had built a flotation machine, and large samples of the soil from each of the main deposits were processed on-site. These yielded impressive results. At the time, this flotation based analysis was fairly ground-breaking stuff. As the principle author of the special study (and noted fish specialist), Alwyne Wheeler wrote,

"As a consequence of the methods of retrieval employed it represents a far more complete record of the fishes consumed or caught by the early medieval inhabitants than has hitherto been available for any site in England".

Part of the study was a comparison between the species represented if fish remains were hand-picked or if the soils were flotated. Six contexts were chosen for this comparison. In the hand-picked samples, only the remains of Cod and Plaice were recovered. When soils from the same contexts were passed through the flotation machine, remains of: Cod, Whiting, Herring, Thornback Ray, Horse Mackerel, Plaice, Flounder, Sole, Eel, Turbot, Ling, Conger and Bass were recovered. That's quite a difference.

The results also showed that both nets and lines of hooks were being used, both inshore and offshore. Numerous large iron fish hooks were recovered during the excavations.

That people were fishing at Great Yarmouth, even as early as the tenth century, was not terribly surprising. Prior to the 14th century, the town's coat of arms had consisted of three silver Herring on a blue background; a clear indication of the value of this species to the local economy. As acknowledgement of the contribution Yarmouth boats had made against a French force in the Battle of Sluys on June 24, 1340, King Edward III allowed the town to combine the fish with his royal lions, creating the distinctive town crest still used today.

I can't stand the smell of fish. Our next door neighbour in Lichfield Road was a shrimp fisherman. He used to boil the horrid things, then lay them out to dry on trestle tables in his back yard. My father, who worked as a refrigeration engineer in one of the major fish processing plants along the river, used to come home smelling of the wretched creatures. However, by the late 1950s the fishing industry was almost dead, my dad got a new job in Warwickshire (working in an ice cream factory – I didn't mind him bringing that home) and we moved to the Midlands.

Much has been written about the fishing industry in Great Yarmouth but there is one sea creature that never gets mentioned, and it was not one you wanted to catch. As kids, we used to swim in the North Sea whenever it was warm enough to expose our pallid skins. Actually, the water never really got warm enough, but we were young and eager and didn't mind a bit of shivering and goose bumps.

There were times though, when swimming was a bit gruesome. If the tide was coming in or if there was a stiff on-shore breeze, the water would be awash with floating debris: bits of toilet paper, condoms, sanitary napkins and things which we called 'blind eels'. We tended to steer away from those.

At the time we lived in Yarmouth the town's sewage was piped out into the sea without any treatment. Even as recently as 1998 *The Telegraph* reported that other than a bit of maceration (forcing it through a ¼ inch mesh to break up the big bits) raw sewage was still being pumped into the sea. Things seem to have changed recently and Great Yarmouth's beaches are now considerably less sewage-soaked than they used to be.

Personally, I think that all that swimming with the blind eels helped me build a rather robust immune system. As they say, 'Whatever doesn't kill you makes you stronger'.

Morningthorpe

The commercial gravel pit at Morningthorpe, south of Norwich, contained a large open area from which gravel had already been extracted, and an almost vertical pit face about 10 metres high. To excavate the gravel the machine operator would drive his bucket into the face of the pit, the gravel would cascade down and he would load it into the hopper machine for sorting. In October of 1974, John Rayner, a machine driver, noticed that two pottery jars had fallen from the edge of the pit on to the loose gravel below. They were clearly ancient. The Norwich Castle Museum was called and before long an emergency excavation was underway.

The jars had been identified as early Saxon, and because some cremated bone had been found with them it was a reasonable assumption that they had come from a cremation cemetery. Such cemeteries are not uncommon in Norfolk. Our house at Spong Farm lay just across the road from one of the most well-known and intensively investigated. The earliest record of people finding pots at Spong is 1711 when something like 150 burial urns were dug from a small area. More sophisticated excavations during the 1970s (in which I participated briefly) added hundreds of pots containing cremations from the hilltop cemetery. It is estimated that around 3000 cremation burials dotted the hilltop.

But it soon became clear that while there was definitely a cemetery at Morningthorpe, it wasn't full of cremations and pots but hundreds of early Saxon inhumation (regular) burials.

The Norfolk Archaeological Unit mounted an immediate rescue excavation while arrangements were made with the pit owners to temporarily avoid that part of the gravel working, and funding was sought from the Department of the Environment. I was away travelling through Turkey and Iran at the time, so missed this part of the project.

Fortunately, over the winter, excavation funding was acquired and an agreement with the pit operators had been reached which allowed full excavation of the undamaged area. It was still going to be a rushed job, but anything was better than nothing.

Once again, Andrew was in charge with Bruce handling the field recording, and Other-Andrew, Jude and I excavating and recording the graves, assisted by a fluctuating number of volunteers. It was tough work. The pit machines had stripped off some of the topsoil, but we were still left with the task of scraping the remaining fragments of topsoil off the surface of the hard, unyielding flint gravel subsoil to expose the grave shafts. We had acres to clear just using hoes, shovels and wheel-barrows.

Whenever someone digs into the ground the contents are thrown on to a heap. The subsoil and the topsoil get mixed together and the texture and colour of the soil that eventually goes back into the hole is forever changed. By scraping the surface of the subsoil, we could see where grave shafts had been dug. Their rectangular outlines were visible as areas of slightly darker ground.

Excavating the individual graves was less exhausting but demanded a high degree of concentration. Because of the acidic nature of the soils there was very little human bone remaining in most of the graves, but there were other things.

In the absence of much skeletal material, we had to rely on the artifacts found with the bodies to determine the gender of the buried individual. In most cases it seemed quite clear (at the risk of being accused of making chauvinist assumptions). Men were often buried with shields, spears, knives, and, in one instance, a sword. Women were buried with large cruciform brooches, strings of amber and glass beads and 'girdle-hangers' - unusual key-shaped objects which may have been symbolic representations of female roles in Saxon society.

Some of the burials contained iron buckles and beautifully decorated and gilded 'wrist-clasps', which, as the name implies, were used to fasten clothing at the wrist. One grave of a young male contained the fragmentary remains of a Lyre - a small musical instrument a bit like a harp. In the absence of full skeletal remains we have no idea how this young man died. Perhaps his playing was so persistent and so bad that the villagers couldn't stand him any longer.

Of course, after 1600 years of lying in the ground, most of the artifacts were in less-than-perfect condition. All that usually remained of the shields, for instance, was the central iron boss, and, if we were lucky, part of the handle with some iron-impregnated wood. Usually, only the blades of the spears and knives were preserved. The lyre consisted of some small fragments of wood with sheet-metal strips and the remains of pins.

By the end of the excavation almost 400 graves or grave-like features (it wasn't always possible to tell when there were no bones or artifacts) had been excavated. Virtually all the artifacts were in need of conservation, the process of cleaning and stabilization, before any analysis or writing could proceed, so, once the excavation was complete, I was back at my drawing desk in Gressenhall.

Pots and Tiles

By now I had become something of a fixture at the Unit. When I wasn't hunched over a drawing board I was out doing emergency fieldwork. Whenever someone reported a find, Andrew and I would respond and would often end up conducting small-scale salvage excavations on our own.

One of the larger projects we undertook as a two-person team was the excavation of part of a medieval moated site in Hempstead, in north Norfolk. The landowner had decided that the lands containing the earthwork remains of a moated manor, which had been pasture for hundreds of years, suddenly needed to be levelled and converted into arable land. At least he gave the archaeologists sufficient notice so that a quick survey of the earthworks could be completed before they were destroyed in the name of progress and efficiency.

Not surprisingly, after the bulldozing, there was plenty of debris lying around on the surface, including many decorated tiles. After poking around a bit the owner discovered that some of the tiles were still in place, and, perhaps feeling a bit sheepish, called the Norwich Castle Museum. That's when we were called in.

During three weeks on site, Andrew and I cleared a large excavation area by hand, exposing a complete section of floor made entirely of impressed and glazed fourteenth century tiles. Although the walls and footings of the original building had long ago been dug out, we were able to map their locations on the basis of the 'robber trenches' which remained.

We also excavated a Saxo-Norman pottery kiln in the village of Bircham and a Romano-British Mortaria (mixing bowl) kiln in Ellingham in South Norfolk, both found during building work and recognized as important by the developers. Andrew generously included me as co-author in the eventual publications even though my part had mainly been excavating and producing the drawings while he did all the research and the writing. It was a good arrangement. We were competent and efficient.

Those days out of the office were often long and tiring, but almost always enjoyable. The kiln in Ellingham had been found by the landowner during construction work on his farm, in November 1976. It was cold, damp and windy, but, because the construction had to continue soon, we had no alternative but to complete the work and put up with the conditions. Andrew and I would drive down early, work all morning, then head to the pub at lunchtime to warm up. The pub offered a particularly strong and tasty winter ale, which warmed our bodies but did little to move the excavation forward.

On the way home, we would often stop to buy a large bottle of cider to swig along the way. Nobody gave much thought to drinking and driving in those days.

The artifacts from the Morningthorpe Saxon cemetery were still being conserved, but, even so, my desk was covered in Saxon goodies. A couple of years before, part of another cemetery had been excavated near the village of Bergh Apton, only a few miles from Morningthorpe. The circumstances of the discovery were remarkably similar: gravel pit, artifacts noticed during digging, emergency salvage.

After some indoctrination at the Norwich Castle Museum, under the watchful and intimidating eye of the Keeper of Archaeology, Barbara Green, I was let loose on the artifacts. The process of archaeological illustration isn't just a case of making a pretty picture that looks a bit like the object. It involves plenty of measurement and a whole lot of interpretation. Key elements of an object might be obscured by corrosion; a drawing can suggest or indicate those elements in a way no photograph can, no matter how crisp or skilfully taken.

Some of the complicated decorated objects such as wrist-clasps, square-headed brooches and ornamental shield mounts would take many hours before something approaching acceptable emerged on the paper. One or two of the larger brooches took days.

My skill never achieved the quality of some of the top-notch professional illustrators, but they were accurate and workmanlike.

But I was restless. I couldn't see myself being content to stay where I was, doing what I was doing forever, no matter how interesting the archaeology or convivial the company. Andrew and Julia had recently married and were looking to move from Spong Farm into their own house. Other-Andrew and Julie had moved to York. Now that the Unit was part of the County Council, the working environment was becoming more formal and constrained. Our world was changing[2].

To clear my head and get a new perspective I jumped on my motorbike and rode down to visit an excavation in Dorchester that was being run by Chris Green, one of the former members of the Norfolk Unit. I met a girl there; a Canadian from Ontario. We got along well, explored Scotland together on my motorbike and before long, I was heading across the Atlantic for a visit.

---

2   *Incidentally, reports on the excavations at Hamwic, Grantham and in Norfolk have all been published.*

CHAPTER 2

CANADA – ROCKS, TREES AND WATER

One day I was hanging around my uncle's house in Toronto, waiting out the last few days before my flight home to the UK, and the next I was heading north on the bus to Sault Ste. Marie thinking, "What have I got myself into?".

As I looked out of the window, all I could see were trees, endless trees, broken only by the occasional splash of blue as we passed a lake or crossed a river, or by some grey rocks, then more trees.

"How am I supposed to look for archaeological sites here?" I wondered, looking out over what appeared to be limitless forest.

"More to the point, how did anyone ever live here – and why?"

As you can tell, I was well-prepared and well-suited for my new job.

During the previous few weeks I'd been in frequent contact with Don MacLeod, then head of the Ontario government's archaeology program. I'd hatched a poorly-considered idea that if I could find a bit of work in archaeology, it would give me the opportunity to stay in Canada for a while longer, spend a bit more time with my girlfriend, and perhaps see some more of the country. I had no idea whether such a thing was possible and was clueless about work permits, visas or whether it was even permissible for someone in the country on vacation to stay and work (it isn't!). After talking myself into some interviews which were false starts and dead ends, I ended up across the desk from Don in his down-town office. I found his salty jokes amusing and that his odd tics and sudden explosive movements didn't bother me at all. We liked each other immediately.

I had been thinking along the lines of a bit of paid work as a digger on an excavation; something where a strong back and a decent work ethic were the primary job requirements, so I was completely floored when Don called me in again a couple of weeks later and described the job he had in mind.

"We need you to do some base-line archaeological survey work to build up an inventory of northern Ontario sites. In the summers, you'll be flown in to the bush by float plane with a canoe, camping gear, another person, and enough food for a couple of weeks at a time. You'll paddle the river and lake shores, test for archaeological sites, record their locations, collect artifacts – that sort of thing. In the winters you'll write up the surveys."

It was a dream job for someone like me. Back in the UK I'd always been an outdoorsy type, spending as much time as I could hiking, camping, climbing, caving and riding my bicycle. I could paddle a kayak; surely I could learn to manage one of those vast, fat Canadian canoes?

There was a bunch of other stuff about assisting the Regional Archaeologist, reviewing development plans and providing resource information to other ministries, but I didn't much listen to that. Then he told me what I would be paid. It was approximately three times what I had been earning in the UK. It's a good thing I was sitting down.

I did briefly wonder how Don thought my prior experience as an archaeological assistant and illustrator in England fitted me for the job he described, but if he was prepared to overlook any suitable Canadian candidates and my lack of paper qualifications I wasn't about to argue. It was only later that I realized that I was hired, not so much for my technical skill, expertise and knowledge, but because Don thought I might be naive or easy-going enough to get along with the guy who would be my boss.

As the bus passed through Sudbury, then rolled west towards 'the Soo', I caught glimpses of the vastness of Lake Huron between the trees. As we passed the surging waterfall at Serpent River, I thought about my first and only attempt at paddling a canoe.

I had spent a little time painting a cottage near Haliburton in exchange for free use. There was a canoe under the deck, so one evening I decided to take it for a spin on the lake. There were two seats. Obviously, a solo paddler didn't sit in the front, so I did what I thought made sense and plonked my backside onto the rear seat. The bow of the canoe immediately lifted clear of the water in a most unsettling way. Hmm..this is going to take a bit of getting used to.

I pushed off from the dock and started to paddle in my best imitation of people I'd seen in old Hollywood movies; stroke on one side, flip the paddle over, stroke on the other. The canoe bobbed disconcertingly, a slight wind caught the bow and the whole canoe immediately swung hard left. In no time I was half way down the lake, out of control and in danger of imminent capsize. Gingerly I moved forwards so my weight was closer to the centre of the canoe. The bow lowered slightly and the boat felt more stable, but now I had to reach too far to get my paddle into the water on either side.

Getting back to the dock was exhausting. For every stroke I made that moved me forward, the wind would push me back almost the same amount. I zig-zagged up the lake in a most erratic manner. Eventually, tired, blistered and sore, I hauled the canoe out of the water, slid it back under the deck and went inside for a beer. There was clearly a bit more to handling a canoe solo than I'd thought.

I was on a steep learning curve during those first few months in Sault Ste. Marie. When we weren't out of town working on some project or other, I spent all my time reading: everything from old fur traders' expedition accounts and books on local geology and history, to endless archaeological journal articles.

I also learned about black flies and mosquitoes. I'd had my first introduction to them while I was painting the cottage. They were fine during the day – little more than a minor irritation – but if I made the mistake of going into town for supplies in the afternoon, the 5 mile walk back in the early evening was torment as they descended in swarms to syphon my poor English blood. I had no resistance to their bites. Each one caused a nasty welt – and there were thousands.

Later that summer, working on excavations at the Northwest Company post at La Cloche on the north shore of Lake Huron, I was driven almost to distraction. The little monsters didn't even wait until they could find exposed flesh: they would bite me right through my jeans, favouring the area just below my buttocks as I bent over in the pits.

I also learned to handle a canoe - properly this time - becoming reasonably adept, whether solo or with another person. Swapping paddle strokes from one side to the other was soon abandoned.

When I wasn't at work, I spent a lot of time exploring. There are innumerable trails leading into the bush near Sault Ste Marie and I hiked many of them. I knew there were supposed to be bears about – I'd even seen one or two crossing the road while driving – but I didn't give them much thought until that fall.

I'd hiked in a few miles on an old logging road leading north from Gros Cap, where Lake Superior narrows at the beginning of the St. Mary's River. It had rained the day before, the footing was a bit loose and my running shoes left clear marks in the mud. Eventually I felt I had gone far enough so I turned around and started to retrace my steps. After about a mile the hair on the back of my neck started to prickle. There were my nice, crisp footprints, but superimposed over them were the unmistakeable prints of a large bear. He'd followed me for a few hundred yards, then, presumably losing interest, turned off the trail and back into the bush.

Having worked on English sites where artifacts were plentiful, stratigraphy was common and rich, sub-surface features were expected, it took a bit of adjustment to get my head around sites where a few stone flakes in what looked like natural soil were all that one might find. My first introduction to these somewhat ephemeral sites was at Mark's Bay, out by the Sault Ste. Marie airport. There was absolutely nothing on the surface to show that the area had been inhabited, but by systematically digging little test pits at regular intervals through the forest we were able to define areas where people had been camped during the Late Archaic period, about 4000 years ago.

The sites were not impressive and nor were the finds. During a whole day of testing, we might come up with little more than a handful of chert flakes. And yet, here was a place people had lived all those years ago. Who were they? What had they been doing there? Why had that place been chosen, when there were so many other places they could have been? How did they survive? In their own way, these ephemeral sites were every bit as interesting as a Roman cross-roads village or a medieval manor.

One day, as we were driving out to Mark's Bay, I asked the others what winter was like. I'd heard that Sault Ste Marie tended to get a fair bit of snow, so pointing to one of the fields I said, 'by mid winter, how much snow will be lying in that field'. I was staggered by the reply, as they all pointed to somewhere around their hips. I'm not sure I really believed them.

I tried to imagine what it must have been like for hunter-gatherer people to survive in those conditions without permanent shelter, and with food they had to catch and prepare themselves. I couldn't.

My first apartment in the Soo had been downtown, but I soon left it for a trailer in a small park in Heyden, about 10 miles north. My relationship with the girl I had met in Dorchester had fizzled out, as such things sometimes do. I wanted to be closer to 'the bush', I wanted a dog, I wanted to heat with wood; in short, I wanted more of the rugged, outdoorsy Canadian experience.

My next door neighbour in the trailer park was a rotund, hearty fellow named Dan. Dan introduced me to the rustic side of life in northern Ontario. He was perpetually out-of-work, filling his time with odd jobs which usually resulted in him not getting paid, but he was always looking for the big scheme which would bring him untold riches. His wife Mae was a feral creature, whom Dan assured me would be really pretty 'if she got her nose straightened and her teeth fixed'. Dan's yard was filled with broken snow-machines, cannibalized pickup trucks and sundry bullet hole perforated appliances, but he was kind and generous with his beer and company. I never had the chance to get lonely or homesick.

Before winter struck, I was sent on my first solo mission as a representative of the Ministry of Culture and Recreation. A Ministry of Natural Resources Conservation officer had noticed that part of the rock face at the Matabitchuan pictographs had spalled off and was lying in the shallows at the base of the cliff. Pictographs are red ochre rock paintings which are found all over northern Ontario, usually on vertical cliffs overlooking lakes or rivers. They are hundreds of years old.

My job was to drive the 300 miles to Temagami, meet up with the MNR staff at their district office, be taken out to the site by truck and boat, and retrieve the rock. It all seemed rather straightforward.

At the Temagami MNR office, I was introduced to my chauffeur for the day – a big, rugged looking guy with a prosthetic leg who, since I can no longer remember his name, I'll call Wayne. Wayne led me out to his truck. An aluminium boat was already strapped on the rack and a motor and fuel were sitting in the bed, so we jumped in, or at least I did, and we set off south of town, heading for the Rabbit Lake Road.

I was still unused to travelling on unpaved roads at highway speeds, so the first few miles of skittering sideways around corners and juddering over washboard were a little unsettling. After a while I grew accustomed to Wayne's driving and relaxed. We must have driven 20 miles or more before we reached a place to unload the boat, during which time we hadn't seen another vehicle. In the process, we had crossed a couple of streams without the benefit of bridge or ford, just by bouncing over the boulders with water not far below the door sills.

We didn't have to travel far to reach the pictograph cliff, easily found the rock spall with the painting and managed to lever the heavy rock into the boat without capsizing. If I'd been a little taken aback by Wayne's missing leg when we started out, I'd long ago forgotten about it. He was immensely capable, handling himself over tricky terrain with confidence and ease.

Wayne had quickly realized that I was a complete neophyte to the Canadian bush as I peppered him with endless questions, so on our way back I think he decided to play a little trick on me. Just after we'd crossed back over one of the streams, he switched off the engine for a smoke and a drink from his Thermos. Other than the sound of the water burbling over the stones and the occasional peep from a bird, it was completely silent.

When he went to start the engine again, the key turned in the ignition but nothing happened; no click, no whirr of the starter, nothing. We sat there for a while and tried again. Nothing.

"Perhaps one of the battery leads has come loose?" I said.

Wayne popped the hood and I took a look. No, both were firmly attached to the battery and there was no sign of any corrosion. He reached for the two-way radio that all MNR trucks carry, but all he could find was static.

"Well, we seem to be stuck?" said Wayne.

I think he was expecting some kind of a reaction from me, but really I wasn't very worried, and in fact was more concerned about his well-being than my own. I knew I could easily jog-walk the 20 miles back to the highway if I had to. I was thinking about the damage he would do to his leg if he tried to walk that far on his prosthesis.

"If you want to stay here, I could walk back out to the highway and get some help, but it's going to take a few hours," I said.

"Let's just give it one more try," said Wayne.

I'll never know whether he had left the truck in Drive deliberately or not, but he snicked the lever to Park, turned the key, and of course the truck started instantly. I have a feeling that he could also have been in contact with his colleagues at the base any time he wanted, but was just finding static for his own amusement and to see how distressed I would be by the idea of being stuck in the bush.

When winter finally arrived it soon became clear that my colleagues had not been exaggerating about the snow. I was astounded by the way it covered everything in a thick blanket, how immense snow banks lined every road and was astonished by the way people continued to drive as if the road surface were bare, and not composed of two inches of hard-packed snow and ice. My own driving was tentative at first, but gradually I got used to the feeling of the car slewing around. I wasn't always completely aware of driving conditions though. On one occasion, heading back to Sault Ste Marie after some meetings in Toronto, I noticed that my speedometer was jumping between 60 to 100 miles an hour and my engine was making odd noises, even though my road speed was steady. It eventually dawned on me that my rear wheels were losing traction, allowing the revs to rise. I slowed down and drove with a bit more caution once I'd clued in.

While I'd been in Temegami, one of the MNR planners had sold me a pair of his old cross-country skis, for next to nothing, so I would be able to get out and enjoy the winter. Buying those skis was one of the best things I ever did.

To the east of my trailer park was a vast, undeveloped area of rocky bush, dotted with innumerable small lakes and ponds. At first I was cautious, sticking to existing snowmobile trails and only skiing during daylight. It didn't take me long before I was venturing out on night time trips, sometimes for many hours, gliding across frozen lakes with trees cracking in the cold like pistol shots. In retrospect, these trips were possibly a bit unwise. I was on my own, often miles from anywhere. If I'd fallen and injured myself or gone through the ice, that would have been a quick, cold end to life in Canada.

My German Shepherd dog Mishi, whom I adopted from the Humane Society in Sault Ste Marie, used to accompany me on these jaunts. Most of the time she was happy to run along behind me as we sped down the trails, but whenever we came to a downhill section and our speed picked up, she viewed it as a race and would try to edge by, even if it meant ploughing through chest deep snow. Usually this was fine, but once in a while she would either edge me off the trail, or step on the skis, sending me flat onto my face on the hard-packed surface. It's a disconcerting feeling to have the wind knocked out of you when you're all alone, it's minus 25, the middle of the night, and you're 5 miles from home.

There was one spot on our regular route where the lake narrowed to a stream, the ice was thin, and flowing water was near the surface. Mishi was usually fairly smart about staying away from thin ice or open water, but one night she ventured too close and fell in. She managed to get her front legs on to some firm ice and I was able to edge close enough to grab her collar and haul her out. I was really worried that she would soon be clad in a rigid suit of ice armour and would freeze. Little did I know about German Shepherd's fur. Even though she had completely submerged, only the guard hairs had got wet. Her skin was still completely dry. I just brushed the ice off her coat, gave her a pat, and carried on.

Towards the end of my first year the work permit that Don had managed to wangle for me was about to run out and I had decided I wanted to stay on. It is not permissible to apply for Landed Immigrant status (as it was then called – now Permanent

Residency) while living in Canada, and I was told, in no uncertain terms by Federal Government officials, that I had to go home and apply from there. Unfortunately for them – fortunately for me - they made the mistake of advertising my job without informing the province. Don pounced on this. Before I really understood what was happening he had berated the Federal officials about crossing jurisdictional lines, they had worked out a compromise, and I had an appointment with the Canadian Consul in Minneapolis. By the time I crossed the border again at Sarnia, I was officially a Landed Immigrant.

In the late 1970s the provincial government was still doing useful things with our taxes. One of these was sponsoring summer training positions in various departments, giving students a chance to earn a little cash while gaining valuable work experience. Each year we were able to hire a small number of 'Experience' students to extend our capacity to do archaeological fieldwork.

One of the students that came looking for a job received an unusual greeting. Even though our offices were in a government building, our dogs were accustomed to coming to work with us. Usually they lay down and were docile and quiet until the end of the day. This time though, when Christine came in looking for a job, Mishi jumped up, knocking her back against the wall. Mishi was just being exuberant, and fortunately Chris was comfortable with big dogs and wasn't shaken or hurt. I think we both felt something pass between us that day. I made sure she got the job; she gladly accepted it.

It soon became apparent that Christine was a skilful canoeist, a competent field worker and virtually immune to the effects of mosquitoes. If we were out hiking together I would be surrounded by a cloud of them; they barely bothered with her at all. She was studying archaeology and history at the University of Western Ontario so the summer job was a perfect fit. We soon teamed up as a survey crew.

One of the jobs we did together was to survey some of the interior lakes just south of Missinaibi Lake Provincial Park. A small group of us had driven in to the park, then been airlifted by Beaver float plane in to Little Missinaibi Lake, just a few miles to the south of the main lake. We were an odd group – half a dozen people with all their digging and camping gear and three dogs. The dogs didn't seem to mind the flight, although hoisting them up into the belly of the plane was a bit of a struggle.

While Thor, the Regional Archaeologist, and the rest of the crew settled down to excavate part of a small Woodland period site by the lake shore, Chris and I paddled away to test some of the many bays for archaeological sites, to record some pictographs and to explore some of the smaller streams and lakes. This was exactly the kind of work Don had described. It was perfect.

At first we slowly cruised the lake shore looking for possible camp sites. In a land of rocky, forested and steeply-sloping shores, the number of places which attract the eye and say 'you could put a tent up here' are surprisingly few. At each location we would clamber on shore, dig some test pits, and sift some soil. If we encountered any fragments of pottery or chips of chert we would intensify our testing, sketch the site, record its location on our maps, then move on. If we didn't, we'd just paddle on to the next place.

Little Missinaibi Lake has many arms, like a gigantic octopus smeared across the landscape. On about our third day, we paddled down one of the narrow arms with a strong breeze at our backs. As the day wore on the wind gradually rose, driving us to the end of the bay. There was no way to fight the wind and waves blowing down the arm. We just had to sit and wait.

You can't fight nature when you're out working in this kind of environment. We soon learned to work long hours when the conditions allowed, and to hunker down, shelter, and wait when they didn't. To do anything else was to court disaster.

The north arm of Little Missinaibi Lake gradually narrows, becoming the Little Missinaibi River flowing north into Missinaibi Lake. That's far too many Missiniabis in one sentence, so I hope you're following. Before the arm of the lake turned into the river, we turned west up a tiny creek heading for Elbow and Trump Lakes.

The creek was narrow, twisty, and choked with vegetation as it found its way through what was really a massive floating bog. Some of the bends were so tight that we had to get out onto the bank and lever the canoe across. The water was rarely more than a foot deep and the colour of tea that's sat too long. Much of the time we were using our paddles as pries, pushing against the banks and the stream bottom, which brought up putrid globs of decaying vegetation. It was hard, sweaty work and we were soon filthy.

After about a mile we entered Elbow Lake. At first, all was quiet, but gradually we could hear the sound of an outboard motor. Eventually a 14 foot fishing boat emerged from around 'the elbow', headed our way and drifted to a stop next to our canoe.

We were truly surprised to it. Unless the boat and it's crew had been flown in, which seemed unlikely, the only way in to Elbow and Trump Lakes was the way we had just come. We'd had a hard enough time in the canoe. The fatter, heavier fishing boat would have been even more of a handful.

The two guys aboard looked to be in their early thirties. They had long hair and bushy beards, and while I can't remember whether they were wearing camo clothing, they should have been to complete the picture. We guessed they were probably Vietnam veterans.

With a big smile and in the broadest southern-States drawl I think I've ever heard, the guy in the front of the boat said,

"Why, you're the first wild folks we've seen."

Beyond the end of Elbow Lake the going got really rough. Although the distance between Elbow and Trump was just a few hundred yards, it was clear that few people ever went that way and no real portage trail existed. Certainly our American friends had not bothered.

Partly dragging and partly carrying the canoe and our gear, we managed to struggle through the swamp and alders, finally emerging on to Trump Lake. It was still, beautiful, and almost completely free of any signs that anyone had been there before. We paddled by a couple of small islands, finally choosing to camp on the large island in the middle of the lake.

By the time we had pitched our tent and started to arrange our supper we were both exhausted, but there was one more thing to do. All the bushes within a step or two of our tent were laden with the most luxuriant crop of perfectly ripe blueberries. If you have never eaten fresh blueberries swimming in evaporated milk, after a long, hard day's paddle, as the sun goes down over a perfect still lake which you have entirely to yourselves, you haven't lived.

After we had finished our work on Trump Lake we retraced our steps and rejoined the main crew on Little Missinaibi Lake in time for the float plane pick up. Thor had arranged the time and place, so we were all packed and ready as the plane flew overhead. We were expecting him to land then taxi in close to the shore, but to our surprise he just kept flying. A few minutes later we heard the distinctive engine sound returning as he flew over again, this time at a much lower altitude. We could see the plane circling the lake for a while longer until finally he landed and coasted in to shore.

"Are you the crew to be lifted out to Missinaibi Lake?" asked the pilot. We assured him we were.

"I didn't think it could be – what about the dogs? I don't think I can take them."

As you can probably tell by now, this was not the same pilot who flew us in. This one was worried that the dogs would panic and become uncontrollable. We assured him that the dogs were coming with us – it was either all of us, or none of us. Of course the dogs just lay down in the back with the baggage. They were getting to be old hands at flying.

We had been in touch with some of the Ministry of Natural Resources staff in the Chapleau district who wanted some information about archaeological sites in the Wenebegon River system to add to their sensitive areas files. After chatting with Jerry, a bit of a canoeing legend in the area, and the only man I've ever seen hoist a full-sized canoe over his head with one hand, we heard that we could paddle in from the Chapleau Road along Burying Creek to get to the lake and river that we wanted to survey.

Jerry was fairly off-hand about the route.

"There are a couple of lift-overs and some riffles, but it's fairly easy going", he'd said.

We should have taken that description with a pinch of salt!

The creek flowed under the road through a culvert, so we parked the car, loaded up the canoe, slipped through the narrow culvert, and headed downstream. The creek was typical of so many northern Ontario waterways, following a winding course through a vast, floating bog. Hundreds of years ago, many of these bogs used to be lakes, but over the years have become choked with dead and dying vegetation. Eventually the bog narrowed and Burying Creek started to look more like an ordinary stream with forest lined banks and a shallow bed of rocks and boulders. It was rarely much wider than the canoe was long.

Chris and I were in the middle of an argument about whose fault it was that we'd just hit a rock, as we rounded a bend. The water was flowing more quickly now and as the current carried us along, we saw what I thought was a large rock right in the middle of the stream.

Chris said, "It's a moose".

"No, it's a rock"

"No, it's a moose"

Then the rock lifted its head, water dripping from its rubbery lips.

"Back-paddle – quick", I said, but Chris needed no helpful suggestions from me and was already doing her best to stop us from drifting right into it. Fortunately, the moose wanted nothing to do with us. She stood up, climbed the bank and melted into the forest.

Not much further along, the stream was choked with fallen trees and brush. It may have been a beaver dam at one time, but the spring floods had piled additional branches against the obstruction. Both of us had to get out, stand on the branches, then heave the canoe across. The trouble was that the branches would slowly sink. By the time we could get back into the canoe we were almost to our waists in water.

Before we reached the lake we had to lift over three or four of these obstructions, each one as tricky and tiresome as the last. We were beginning to have dark thoughts about Jerry's 'couple of lift-overs'.

That evening, we camped on a small island. Within minutes of arriving we noticed chert flakes, fire-cracked-rock, and tiny fragments of native pottery eroding from the well worn area used as a camp site by fly-in fishermen.

Over the next few days we excavated a small part of the site. As we were working we heard the distinctive sound of a helicopter approaching. To our surprise, it landed immediately adjacent to our site (it was on floats) and an Ontario Provincial Policeman and a Ministry of Natural Resources Conservation Officer got out.

I had assumed they had seen our nice, tidy rectangular holes and were wondering what we were doing, and whether it was legal. But no, they didn't have the slightest curiosity on that score – they only wanted to know if we had been illegally fishing (which we hadn't). Within minutes they were gone.

That evening, Chris, Mishi and I jumped into the canoe, and as the sun started to go down, we paddled into the large bay on the east side of the lake. As we slowly drifted in, we could hear a strange, rhythmic slopping noise coming from the bush which grew steadily louder. Eventually the cause came in view. Four female moose, shadowed by a large male with a magnificent set of antlers, emerged at the lake shore, waded into the water, and started feeding in the water lilies.

By this time Mishi was quivering with excitement and making little whining sounds. This seemed to encourage the moose and they started to swim in our direction. We quickly backed up until we thought we were at a safe distance, then watched until the light was nearly gone. The moose continued to graze as we turned the canoe for our island and left them to feed in peace.

After finishing our work on the lake, Chris and I paddled south on the Wenebegon River, seeing moose and otters on the river bank and camping at a delightful waterfall on our way. If it all sounds a bit magical, it's because it was.

After about 30 miles the river swings within 500 metres of the Chapleau Road, and a narrow gravel track connects the two. We hauled our canoe and gear up from the river and I left Chris and Mishi while I walked out to the road and hitch-hiked back to collect the car which was parked at Burying Creek. By the time I got back a couple of hours later, Chris's neck was a mass of purple welts. The black flies had been busy.

Of course, it's not always canoeing and black fly season in northern Ontario. Winter brings its own collection of joys and hazards which we seemed perfectly placed to experience. This next little section falls into the category of "What were you thinking, you bloody idiots?"

We had heard that a set of previously unreported pictographs had been noticed on a rock face along a small river somewhere between Shining Tree and Gowganda. Mid-winter seemed the perfect time to look for them. We could ski in and photograph and trace the paintings while standing on the ice. That was the plan anyway.

The new ministry GMC Suburban truck was available, so we loaded up our skis and camping gear and started the six hour drive. Once we found the general area we parked the truck, unloaded and started to ski in. It was bitterly cold and the light was fading fast, so we chose a spot at the edge of a forestry clear-cut and put up our tent.

At first it was rather fun. The air was incredibly still and clear, the stars were out in profusion and we were warm from the exertions of skiing. But gradually, everything started to fall apart. Part of the reason for camping at the edge of the clear-cut was there would be plenty of dry wood close by. We gathered some up then I started a fire - or at least I tried to. Every time I got a little blaze going it was as if a giant frigid hand reached down and snuffed it out. After numerous attempts I conceded defeat and tried plan B.

Our little camp stove relied on lighting a bit of fuel, then pressurizing the tank to produce a robust blast that would boil a pot of water in a couple of minutes. Once again, something about the cold that night got in the way. Perhaps it was too cold for the fuel to vaporize. Whatever I tried to do was unsuccessful. We had been hoping to cook ourselves a meal and make some hot chocolate but we now had to abandon that plan too.

By this point both Chris and I were starting to get cold. Even Mishi, who was usually immune, couldn't wait to get inside the tent and curl up on the sleeping bags. With no fire and no supper other than some cold salami, we retreated, fully dressed, into our sleeping bags, settled Mishi between us, pulled up our hoods and tried to stay warm.

It was a long, cold night. Our sleeping bags were rated to about -15c but it was far, far colder than that. Mishi had her nose tucked in. She gave off plenty of heat so we curled around her and she kept us from freezing.

I imagine we must have slept for part of the night, probably in short bursts, but eventually, after an age, there was a little light in the sky. We stayed put until the sun rose over the trees, hoping that it would provide a little warmth as we hastily packed our gear and got moving again.

I was convinced that if we started skiing towards the pictographs, the exercise and the sunlight would soon warm us up. I was wrong. After only a few hundred yards I turned to see how Chris was faring, and was shocked to see that her nose and both cheeks were completely frozen.

"You've got frost bite" I said. "We'd better head back."

"So have you," Chris mumbled through chilled lips.

It was probably a good thing that we hadn't skied in very far the previous evening, as by the time we got to the truck we could barely move. Our muscles were tight, and by now our hands and feet were numb. It's a reasonable assumption that our brains weren't working too well either – although some might say they weren't working too well before we set off. Even Mishi was starting to lift her feet and look uncomfortable.

I fumbled with the key, managed to unlock the doors and we staggered inside, where it was every bit as cold as outside. I put the key in the ignition and turned it. The brand new ministry truck grunted and the engine grudgingly made one sluggish rotation. I let the key go, gave it a couple of seconds, then tried again. This time the engine spun fractionally faster, then burst into life. I have rarely been more relieved.

As soon as we got into the truck our breath froze on the inside of the windscreen, so we sat with the engine running for a few minutes to clear it. As the heat worked its way through the cabin, and finally to us, our feet, hands, and faces throbbed and ached almost unbearably.

For years I've been telling people that we heard on the radio that it had been -46c that night. Now I'm not so sure – that might have been with wind-chill factored in. I recently checked winter temperatures for around that time and the lowest I can find is -43c, with some winter nights down to the low -30s. Whatever the real temperature was, it was dangerously cold.

We drove straight to a motel in Chapleau and stayed there for the next two days, sick with headaches, chills, and upset stomachs. We had learned an important lesson about winter camping: unless you really know what you're doing and have all the right equipment, it's darned dangerous. Oh yes – and take a big dog – she might save your life!

Mishi was a constant companion on most of our work trips. She could usually be relied on to behave herself, although she did manage to bite the same Park Superintendent twice. Ray was a loud and blustery guy, always in uniform, whom I might have been inclined to bite myself had he not been so generous with ministry equipment and resources. Actually, now I think about it, the uniform may have been the trigger, since she also once nipped a policeman who had come to our door to investigate a car accident nearby. Fortunately, both Ray and the cop were wearing high leather boots, so her attentions to their ankles were little more than a squeeze. Most of the time though, she was calm and reliable and would accept being petted by strangers – although always with the disdain typical of the breed.

During a work trip on Lake Temagami, Mishi was lying quietly in the bottom of the fishing boat we had rented as we headed up one of the lakes long arms. Owen was in the prow, Chris was in the middle, and I was in the rear. As Mishi relaxed, her front legs slid beneath the centre seat and the instant she wanted to move, the sharp edge of the folded aluminium bit deeply into her foreleg. With a yelp she struggled to her feet, blood spurting in all directions, spraying our packs, ourselves, and mixing with the oily water in the bottom of the boat. Chris immediately grabbed her and stuck her thumb in the wound, as I headed the boat for shore about half a mile away. She was still losing blood fast – we wondered whether we'd even be able to save her.

On shore Chris tore up her shirt and tied a tourniquet above the wound, which slowed the bleeding. Owen jumped back into the boat and headed up the lake with instructions to find someone who might be able to help, while I dug out our fishing gear.

The cut had gone in at an angle, leaving a large flap of flesh over the severed artery. Using a barb-less fish hook and some fine nylon line, I tried to stitch it closed. Mishi didn't complain at all – I think she was either in shock, or dopey from losing so much blood, but my attempts were futile and ineffective.

By this time, constant pressure on the wound and the slowing effect of the tourniquet had reduced the blood flow to a seep, and it was no longer spurting.

After a while, Owen returned with news that he'd found help at a cottage just up the lake shore, so we carefully loaded her into the boat again, and after a short, anxious boat ride, landed at the cottage where a vacationing doctor from Pennsylvania was waiting to help. He quickly examined the wound, decided because the blood around the fleshy flap was already starting to congeal, that stitches weren't necessary, and applied a proper pressure bandage.

It seemed he regularly had to perform minor medical acts during his vacation – usually removing errant fish hooks, or binding up sprains and cuts – but this was the first time he'd had to perform on a dog. We had to sign his medical visitor's book on Mishi's behalf.

That evening we were treated to a delicious supper with the doctor and his family, and a little too much free beer. At one point, Owen started to describe one of our expeditions to a remote community in northern Ontario where we stayed in a "little Jerkwater town". There was a moment of stunned silence before conversation continued. I don't think Owen had any idea what he had just said was distasteful.

Mishi, however, lay quietly on the floor, well fed and content, as if the drama of the day had never happened.

CHAPTER 3

IT DOESN'T SEEM SO STRANGE ANYMORE

1980 was a busy year. Chris and I got married in April, then left for Saskatoon on our honeymoon. Saskatchewan's largest city might seem a strange destination, but I had signed up to give a talk at the annual Canadian Archaeological Association conference which was being held there that year, so we combined the two events.

Over the previous winter I had spent most of my time examining and analyzing the Middle Woodland pottery from excavations at the Whitefish Island site; a large fishing settlement right at the rapids of the St. Mary's River in Sault Ste Marie. I knew my stuff, my slides were prepared, I thought I was ready.

After sitting through some other related papers, it was my turn. It started out well enough; I described the site, its important geographical location, the nature of the excavations, showed my pottery slides, then gradually, embarrassingly, ground to a halt. I hadn't prepared a structure or formal talk; I had assumed I could just get by on what I knew. I was wrong. One or two of the more eminent archaeologists in the audience (Ron Mason and Jim Wright) bailed me out with helpful questions, but it was a bit of a disaster.

I have given many public talks since, but have always made

sure to be fully prepared. Even when it seems as though I'm speaking extemporaneously, I have notes and headings available for when I falter. Some lessons take a long time to learn. This one I learned in an instant.

It was also the year that I decided that despite the benefits of a decent salary and some job security, it was time to leave my government job. There were many reasons for this, but let's just say that I was perhaps a little less naive and easy-going than Don had hoped.

It began to seem that making a living as an archaeological consultant was a possibility. Government departments were doing less and less active field research, while development companies were being required to check for sites before construction. Even during my last year with the ministry, I'd noticed that our work had been changing; we were doing more project review and less outside work. It was time.

Despite a slow start and periods of dire poverty, I was able to pick up some contract work. Much of it was dull, testing areas where there was little possibility of finding anything to fulfil development agencies' regulatory requirements. Occasionally, though, a peach would come along.

Nakina Lakes

The ripest peach was a contract to survey a group of large lakes in northern Ontario for the Ministry of Citizenship and Culture, funded by the Ministry of Northern Affairs. At the time of the survey (1983), the new Ogoki Road was being extended as a joint project between Ontario and Kimberley Clark – one of the major forestry companies in the province. The new road passed close to a string of large lakes, which, only a few years before, had been reachable only by float plane or a by a long canoe trip. Easy access brings more people. People bring garbage and they don't often take it away again, they cut new paths, they put up shelters, they erode the ground surface, – in short, the landscape is no longer as pristine as it once was.

Despite the immensity of northern Ontario, people always seem to gravitate to the same few places on the landscape. Increased use brings soil erosion and artifact looting. Archaeological sites were at risk. Our job was to find and document some of them before their ruin.

Chris and I left the car where the Ogoki Road crosses the Kawashkagama River. As we parked, we noticed that the two truck campers parked in the same area had been broken into. The rear door of one had been torn right off and the window screens were shredded. We looked into them and saw that a bear had had a grand time once he got inside. Sleeping bags were ripped, boxes and coolers had been torn into, and other less-obvious food items, such as propane cylinders, had been given a playful nip. Chris picked up an insulated coffee mug displaying a deep canine tooth imprint. We hoped we would come across the truck owners so we could prepare them for how badly their vehicles had been trashed.

It was a four mile trip down the river to Abamasagi Lake, through three small sets of rapids, only one of which was marked on our 1:50,000 scale map. Bill, who was managing the project on behalf of the ministry, had loaned us a 17 foot Grumman square stern aluminium canoe and a 4 horsepower motor. I detest aluminium canoes - they are unwieldy and noisy - and I like outboard motors even less, but we had work to do and the motor would allow us to cover distance more quickly than paddling.

Aluminium canoes also tend to stick on rocks. We found this out as we attempted to navigate the first set of rapids. We hit a submerged rock, the heavily-laden canoe immediately swung broadside to the water, and the gunnel dipped menacingly close to the waves. Fortunately, the current continued to swing the canoe in an arc, freeing it from the rock and allowing us to gather ourselves for the rest of the downstream trip. It was an inauspicious start.

Abamasagi Lake is about 12 miles long and almost 3 miles across at its widest point. It was late in the day when we arrived, so we edged down the southern shore for a short distance and found a pleasant-looking clearing behind a low rock shelf where most of the shoreline trees had been cut down by a beaver. Even before we had unloaded everything from the canoe, Chris found a couple of chert flakes on the surface. We'd been on the lake a few minutes and already found our first site.

An inscription carved into the beaver stump just in front of our campsite read,

"Yea, though I walk through the valley of the shadow of death, I will fear no evil. John 1980". Somebody seemed to have been having a tricky time on the lake.

That night the beaver expressed his annoyance with us by swimming around just off shore, then slapping his tail and diving if any of us moved. This drove Mishi wild, but eventually even she settled down and ignored him.

Over the next couple of days we cruised the lake shore, testing suitable spots and recording a few previously undiscovered pre-ontact First Nations campsites, eventually ending up at the western end of the lake where we could see clear signs that we were not alone. As we cruised closer for a look, we met a couple of fishermen. We explained about the truck break-ins and handed over our one piece of evidence. At first they were a bit suspicious, one of the guys even thinking that it might have been Mishi that had bitten the cup, but eventually they realized we were telling the truth and invited us for tea.

In retrospect, I suppose I should have been more cautious. Here we were, alone with half a dozen middle-aged guys in the middle of nowhere, many miles from the nearest people and at least 30 miles from the nearest town. And let me tell you, Chris was pretty darn cute, and since it was hot, not wearing all that much clothing.

By good fortune, the guys were absolute gentlemen. They made us tea and listened politely and with apparent interest while we told them what we were doing, then, since it was getting towards evening, invited us to stay for supper, laughing at the notion that we would be consuming food they may need for themselves.

"We're having walleye." they said. "We catch what we need when we need it".

They must have seen the incredulous looks we exchanged, because in no time we were out in a boat, a few hundred yards off-shore, watching them reel in fish after fish.

I'm not much of a fish-eater. Indeed, if it smells of fish at all, I have no stomach for it, but even I had to concede that freshly-caught walleye, battered in Aunt Jemima pancake mix, served with instant mashed potatoes and washed down with beer, is a pretty fine supper.

Some of the guys had been coming to the same place for

seventeen years. At first they had been flown in, but after the Ogoki Road had been built, they had been able to drive themselves. They clearly loved the place for the quiet, the clean water, the abundant fish, the wildlife (we'd seen a massive, almost jet black moose while we were out in the boat) and for the contrast to the streets of Detroit or Cleveland or wherever else it was they came from. But here's the amazing thing. As we ate, Chris and I couldn't help noticing the enormous pile to broken bottles and rusty cans just to the rear of their camp area. In all those seventeen years, they had brought in enormous quantities of supplies, yet they can't have taken out a single bag of garbage when they left.

Eventually we had to leave our generous, if messy hosts and head back down the lake. A light, steady breeze had been blowing from the west all day, but since we were at the extreme west end of the lake, the water was sheltered and calm. As we moved away from the shore, the waves started to get bigger, rolling in exactly the direction we were heading. At first it was terrific fun. Using the little 4 horsepower motor, we could match our speed to the rollers, surfing the tops of the waves. But as we got further down the lake and the waves continued to build, joining with cross waves from the north, we suddenly realized that we had left fun far behind. If we continued surfing, we would risk capsizing. If we slowed down too quickly, the waves would overtake us and swamp the canoe from the rear.

For once, Mishi was content to lie still in the bottom of the canoe. Chris and I lowered our centre of gravity by kneeling, knees spread as widely as we could for balance and control, while I gradually steered the canoe into slightly less vigorous water closer to the lake shore. We were mightily relieved when we made it back to our campsite safely.

My field notes for the next day are as follows: '*Awoke to the most unbelievably menacing sunrise (if such a thing can exist) and wind. The lake is too rough for travel*', so we stayed put and excavated a few squares at the beaver campsite. We were starting to understand what John 1980 was getting at.

The excavation units contained numerous chert flakes, fire-cracked rock from ancient hearths, and a surprisingly large number of flakes which had been modified for use as cutting tools and scrapers. Unfortunately, within the small area we tested there were no diagnostic artifacts and no ceramics, so it was not possible to say whether the site was Archaic or Woodland without excavating a larger area. But we were there to survey, and had much more terrain to explore once the weather allowed.

It's probably worth pointing out here that even quite ancient sites in northern Ontario – as much as 8000 or 9000 years old - often lie right at, or immediately below the thin topsoil. Soil accumulation is desperately slow in the cold climate and falling spruce needles don't build soil quickly.. A few clod-hopper fishermen scraping an area level to put up a temporary plywood cabin or digging a shallow trench around a tent, can soon degrade a site, wrenching artifacts from where they had originally been dropped, often thousands of years before.

The next day dawned clear and calm, so after a quick breakfast we headed to a spot on the south shore, close to where the river joins the lake. It was an ideal camp site; nice and level, high enough above the water to be dry, and exposed enough to the wind to be relatively insect-free. That's what we thought at first, anyway.

Within our first couple of test pits we determined that this was indeed a place where many people had camped in the past. The topsoil contained beer caps and some small brass nails – the kind used in canoe building. Below that, we found chert flakes and fire cracked rock from ancient camp fires, but more importantly, we saw that this site contained multiple layers of occupation separated by layers of clean sand. Since stratified sites are extremely rare in northern Ontario we decided to excavate a single one metre square unit to give us a proper look at the stratigraphy.

I won't bore you with a blow-by-blow description of the excavation, but as work proceeded we discovered an intact 18th century horizon containing numerous fragments of bones from meals, a butcher's knife similar to many found in excavations at Fort Michilimackinac, and a barbed bone harpoon.

Further down, and separated by a layer of clean sand from the layer below, we found numerous animal bone fragments, chert flakes and flake tools. In an adjacent test pit, in a corresponding soil layer, we found a rim sherd of 'Oneota' pottery, dating to about A.D. 1000. Below yet another layer of clean sand we found more chert flakes and part of a large stone spear-point or knife from the late Archaic period and about 3000 years old.

These were exciting discoveries, but were not acquired without our share of suffering. We were tormented by black flies: those nasty little beasts that settle on you, steal a small chunk of flesh and leave some of their toxic juices behind. Every so often, the torment would get to be too much. We would jump in the canoe, fire up the motor and go for a quick spin around the bay to shed the rotten things. We did much of our note writing while sitting in the canoe.

The long eastern arm of the lake was still unexplored territory for us, so the following day we headed down that way. The lake rapidly narrowed and the bay was lined with steeply-sloping jack-pine-covered rocky shores. We tested numerous places but found nothing. As we worked our way back towards the main body of the lake, we had to fight an increasingly strong wind, and waves which smacked the front of the canoe. The little 4 horsepower motor pushed us along quite well, but the prow of the canoe smashed into each wave, jarring and soaking us.

At first we ventured out into the lake, but it very quickly became clear that to try to proceed was unwise. We would only need to misjudge one wave and we would be flipped in an instant. We cautiously headed back to a small clump of rocks by the shore where we secured the canoe and thought about our next move.

Behind us; swampy forest. Ahead of us; dangerous wind and waves. We had no choice other than to stay exactly where we were. From our rock, we could just about see our tent on the far shore but there was no way to reach it. We were stuck so we settled in for a long wait. There were plenty of mosquitoes to keep us company, but we bruised some sage-willow leaves and rubbed our exposed skin. It seemed to help. Perhaps it was a placebo.

Six hours later the sun started to go down, the wind diminished, and the waves seemed less threatening. Our tent was still visible across the lake, illuminated by the setting sun, almost mocking us. We hustled Mishi into the canoe, settled ourselves on our knees, pulled the motor into life and set off. It was a bumpy, wet ride, but we made it back without incident.

A few weeks later we were back in the area, continuing our work on another massive lake. Esnagami is large by any standard, with a surface area of 27 square miles, more than 60 miles of convoluted shoreline and dozens of islands. Once again, we were using the canoe and motor. Once again the waves were giving us trouble.

While we'd been sitting on that rock on Abamasagi Lake I'd given the problem a bit of thought. Polynesians managed to turn their narrow, tippy dug-out canoes into ocean-going vessels. Why couldn't we do the same? All we needed was something to act as a pontoon, a couple of spruce saplings as supports, and a bunch of rope to lash it all together.

At one of the fishing camps I found a 6 foot length of old plank. We cut a couple of saplings and scrounged some heavy duty cord from one of the islands where someone had used it for a clothes line.

The main difficulty was setting the whole thing up so that the front of my 'pontoon' didn't dig into the water but just skimmed the surface when we were trimmed and level. After a few false starts we had it rigged. It was time to test it out.

Instant, amazing success! In smooth water, the pontoon slipped across the surface with no apparent effect on the speed or handling of the canoe. In rougher water, waves would still throw spray from the bow, but the whole vessel was infinitely more stable. The waves just slid by. We could navigate in water that previously had us at a standstill and even stand up and move around with no likelihood of tipping. It was revolutionary.

We didn't have any more trouble with the waves on Esnagami but it didn't mean that we were in for an easy time. Our base camp for work at the eastern end of the lake was on a lovely little rocky island. Each day we set out to work, returning late in the day to cook supper and sleep. Our days seemed endless. The sun didn't set until after 9.30PM. It was still light until well after 10PM and light again before 6 the next morning.

We had been rather lucky with the weather for the first couple of days. My notes record '*It has been hazy, humid, hot and dead still. Little bother from bugs. Flat water. 5 degrees cooler would be nice, but not too bad*'. The next day though, was different. We awoke to menacingly dark skies. We decided we had enough time to sneak in some work before the weather broke.

Northern Ontario summers can be hot, and with so much water sitting in the lakes and rivers, it's not too surprising that from time to time storm clouds gather. And gathering they were. The air gradually became worryingly still as a mass of dark grey cloud settled overhead.

"I think we'd better head back" said Chris. I didn't need any convincing.

With the motor running flat out, we were skimming across the still lake at top speed when the storm broke. Lightning hit the water between the canoe and the shore with a deafening clap of thunder. Fearful that the next strike would hit us, we raced for the island, and all three of us scuttled into the tent just as the squall hit. At least the island had trees taller than we were. On the water, we were the best target for miles around.

Our engagement with Zeus and his arrows was not over. For the next few days the atmosphere was quiet. We had moved our camp on to a little rocky peninsula so we could complete our survey at the west end of the lake. At first all was well, but the heat and humidity were rising steadily and by nightfall of the third day it had again reached breaking point.

Chris, Mishi and I huddled in our little tent as lightning and thunder burst all around and torrents of rain came thrashing down. The storm didn't really reach its full strength until it was completely dark. One moment it would be pitch black; the next it would seem like daylight, as lightning hit somewhere close by and our ears were stunned by the thunder. Mishi had never exhibited any anxiety about thunder before, but now she lay quivering between us.

Gradually, the sound and light would move further and further away. We would count the time between lightning and thunder claps: two seconds,.....three seconds,.......five seconds,......seven seconds...... and then, disturbingly, five seconds.........three seconds.......two seconds, then the storm would be all around us again.

All night long, the storm rolled around the lake, seeming to leave us, but then returning just as scarily as before. The lashing rain created rivulets of water that found their way under the tent, soaking our sleeping bags and adding a layer of misery to our fear. I don't think any of us slept a moment that night.

It was early October before we started the final part of the fieldwork. Stone Lake is the least accessible of the six we were testing. It drains north by the Kapikotongwa River towards the Albany River and James Bay. Other than an arduous and infrequently used portage from Ara Lake, there were no easy ways to get there.

Fortunately, in those days the various northern government departments still felt some kinship, so Bill was able to arrange a flight for us with the Ministry of Natural Resources. All we had to do was to get ourselves to the plane dock on Kenogamisis Lake near Geraldton and we would be hoisted over to Stone Lake in one of the ministry's float planes.

Since Stone Lake is relatively small, we opted to take our own canoe and save the bother and extra weight of lugging a motor and fuel with us. The ministry's yellow Dehavilland Turbo Beaver was ready at the dock. Once Gary the pilot arrived, we hoisted Mishi in to the cargo bay, threw in our packs and paddles, and watched helplessly as Gary strapped our canoe to the pontoon with two enormous webbing straps. As you can imagine, having a canoe flapping around on the underside of a plane really isn't on, but when he ratcheted the buckles I could hear the fibreglass creaking and complaining. We wondered whether our poor canoe would survive.

It's always a revelation to be inside a small working aircraft. We are so used to the padded luxury of modern automobiles that the stark utilitarian nature of bush planes is a bit of an assault on the senses. They are all about function: simple instruments, a few levers and straps, no padding or concessions to comfort anywhere. The smell and the noise are profound.

With the engine whining and the prop spinning, we cast off and taxied downwind for a few hundred yards before turning. After a couple of quick checks and a word in his radio, Gary pushed the throttle, the noise increased exponentially, the plane raced forwards, slapping across the tops of the waves, and just as I was sure we were going to run out of space, we were in the air and climbing fast.

In four months of work, we had become accustomed to seeing the area by road and water. From the air, we could see that the roads threaded their way along the few eskers and moraines which provided the higher ground. Virtually everything else was water, swamp or swampy forest.

I expect Gary had bearings and a flight plan to follow, but he still relied on a topographical map on his knee to identify his exact location. After about an hour we began to recognize the shapes of the lakes below and could see the Ogoki Road. As Stone Lake became visible we started to lose a little altitude and Gary asked where we wanted to land. Most of the south shore is low and swampy while the north shore is more rocky and rugged. The best spot seemed to be a small sandy bay at the east end of the lake.

MNR pilots usually have vast experience flying their planes into tricky spots in all kinds of conditions, so I'm sure what he did next seemed entirely normal to him. Before we could steel ourselves, he'd dropped a wing, spun the plane in a big, stomach-lurching arc and in moments we were gliding along the water towards the sandy shallows.

We confirmed our pick-up day of the following Friday with Gary, who told us that Friday would be the end of their flying season. We unloaded the canoe, dog and gear and said goodbye. Once again, we were alone, miles from anywhere, completely dependent on our own resources. There were a couple of cabins for fly-in fishermen on the lake, but they were deserted. It was late in the season; we didn't expect to see anyone and we weren't disappointed.

Stone Lake turned out to be a bit of a bust. We did manage to locate some archaeological sites, but we got the impression that with so many larger and more easily accessible lakes close by, Stone hadn't attracted much more than occasional and sporadic use in the past.

Towards the end of the week, the weather turned cold and miserable. We had finished our work ahead of time, so we took advantage of one of the empty cabins and enjoyed a day of relative luxury. These cabins contain nothing of value and are typically left open so that they can be used in emergencies. We just slept on the bunks instead of putting our tent up again, and read the few books and magazines that had been left by the previous occupants, one of whom had left his business card on the table. Astonishingly, he was an archaeologist from Minnesota.

After the fieldwork was over, I contacted him to see if he had noticed anything of cultural value, but he had been there for the fishing and not to find old rocks.

We awoke the next morning to a dull cool day. The sun was completely hidden behind thick, low cloud which reached down to the tops of the trees and muffled all sound. We had no clear idea when the plane might arrive, but it was obvious it would not be soon. Nobody could possibly fly through that cloud.

But we had a problem. It was the Friday before the Thanksgiving long weekend, and as Gary had said, the end of MNR's flying season. If we didn't get picked up that day, at the very least we would have to stay all weekend, and perhaps even have to find our our own way out. We had run out of dog food, our own supplies were running low, and apart from anything else, we'd had enough; we were ready for home, a chance to catch up on paying some bills, a comfortable bed, and something to eat that wasn't freeze dried or irradiated.

The day wore on and the cloud showed no inclination to lift. We ate our remaining few crackers with what was left of the peanut butter. Mishi had to do without. By mid-afternoon, the cloud base had risen slightly, leaving a thin band of clear sky just above the tree tops. Our ears were tuned for the slightest sound, but for hours all had remained quiet.

Then, miraculously, we heard the unmistakeable sound of an air plane. We hurried to consolidate our gear by the water's edge, but as the plane finally came into view, we saw that it wasn't yellow, it wasn't heading our way, and, incredibly, it had wheels, not pontoons. We had no idea where he was going. As far as we knew, it was all lakes and trees for hundreds of kilometres in any direction. Perhaps one of the remote First Nations villages further north had an air strip – we certainly hoped so.

As the sound of the plane gradually disappeared, we began to resign ourselves to a long, hungry weekend. We could feed Mishi on fish – assuming we could catch some – we'd done it before, although she'd given us the most reproachful looks until hunger got the better of her. As for us, we had just enough bits and pieces to keep us going.

Just as we started to haul our gear back up to the cabin, we heard another plane. At first we though it might have been the same one, heading back to somewhere with a landing strip, but the sound got louder and louder until the bright yellow MNR plane emerged out of the narrow band between trees and clouds and dropped down on to the water.

It was a different pilot. He jumped down, said hello, then started to load our canoe. I said something about difficult flying conditions and he laughed.

"These are the days that turn my hair grey", he said, taking off his cap. His head was covered in short, bright red hair – not a grey hair in sight.

It's an eerie feeling to be skimming along just above the tree tops, with a thick, grey opaque matte above. If we went any higher, we were immediately enveloped in heavy mist which cut visibility to virtually nothing. If we'd gone any lower, we would have been trailing the floats across the upper branches. We were probably a couple of hundred feet above the trees, but they felt much closer.

I have often wished that Ontario had a bit more varied topography. A few decent hills or the odd mountain or two wouldn't go amiss. But this wasn't one of those times. For once I was glad that the landscape was relatively flat and there were no rocky precipices looming unexpectedly out of the mist.

While we're coasting along between the treetops and the clouds, I'll take a few moments to tell you another little tale that illustrates the calm and skill of these MNR bush pilots. During another work trip, Chris and I, and probably Mishi too, had been collected from Nagagami Lake for a short flight back to the provincial park on nearby Nagagamisis Lake. I think it was in one of the ministry's older non-turbo Beavers. As we were flying along I noticed the pilot tapping one of the gauges from time to time, which was resolutely stuck on zero. Since he didn't seem terrifically concerned, neither was I. As we banked in for our landing approach, he reached to his side and started pumping a lever. After we'd landed and were taxiing towards the dock, I asked him what the tapping and pumping was all about.

"Oh, the hydraulics for the ailerons had packed up. I was pressurizing them by hand."

Mishi

Most of the time Mishi could be relied on to stay fairly still in the canoe. She was usually content to lie down with her head resting on the gunnel, watching the world go by as we did all the work. But at around 100lbs, when she did move it had an impact. If she was lying with her back to the left, we had to shift right in our seats to compensate and keep the canoe level. If she flopped over to the other side, we would have to adjust again. It was a small price to pay for her company and the knowledge that we would be kept safe from prowling beavers and food-stealing raccoons.

Her presence in the canoe wasn't always entirely welcome though. As we were working our way down the Spanish River, we decided to put her on the shore while we ran a particularly long and tricky set of rapids. Usually she was able to keep pace with the canoe until we found an eddy and loaded her again. This time though, the river was swift, the shoreline was composed of large boulders which made running difficult, and we were soon far ahead. Once we were out of the rapid, I looked back to see her head bobbing down the middle of the canoe channel in the roughest standing waves. She'd obviously tired of trying to make her way along the shore and had taken the path of least resistance.

Very early on in our relationship, while Chris was still at university in London, I concocted a weekend plan. She would fly up to Sudbury, and then we would drive north up to the Onaping River for a couple of days of canoeing. The Onaping appealed to me because it was relatively accessible, had plenty of white-water and was in an area that neither of us knew too well. I met her at the airport and within a couple of hours we were on the river.

Chris had an anthropology assignment due the following Monday, but never being one to let a little thing like that get in the way of an adventure (or a weekend with her boyfriend, for that matter), wrote some of it on the plane and the rest of it while we dried out around the camp fire.

Chris insists she told me it was a ledge, and not a runnable rapid - perhaps I wasn't listening - anyway, we were wedged in the middle of a rapid on a rock shelf when Mishi took the unexpected notion to stand up on the gunwale, immediately dumping us all into the water. I bounced down the rest of the rapids on my belly, trying to keep pace with the canoe. Chris and Mishi, along with all our gear, ended up in an eddy close to the shore. We were unhurt and soon able to retrieve all our stuff and nothing was lost or damaged, but it was a little inconvenient.

Mishi may have been surprised to find herself in the water, but it was of no consequence to her, as she dried off almost immediately. It was a bit more of an issue for us: the water was cold, we were soaked through, we were miles from help (had we needed it), it was late October, and it was just beginning to snow.

Fortunately, there was plenty of dry wood around, I had waterproof matches, and was in the habit of keeping a few strips of birch-bark in my pack, so we soon had a good fire going. What could have been a minor disaster turned out to be a very enjoyable evening. I have a photograph of Chris, sitting between the camp fire and a large rock, with Mishi curled up next to her, while she worked on her anthropology assignment.

The next morning we resumed our paddling. It was a perfect, early winter day. There was a chill to the air, but the water was so still that it was almost impossible to distinguish reflection from real landscape. The canoe glided effortlessly over the water.

We carefully made it through a few more rapids, and had just rounded a bend when saw an enormous male moose carcass hanging from a tree, some tents, and a slowly-smoking camp fire. We had forgotten that our trip coincided with the opening of moose hunting season. From that moment on, we banged our paddles on the gunwales each time we came to a bend in the river, just to make sure we weren't mistaken for a meaty ungulate.

After the trip, I dropped Chris back at the airport, and she got the plane south while I drove west to Sault Ste. Marie. She finished her assignment on the plane. She probably got an 'A'. She usually did!

Years later, when Mishi was already grey muzzled and old, we brought our first child, Sam, home from the hospital and placed him in a wooden crib on the floor. Mishi ambled over, stuck her great big nose right under his backside, almost flipping him over, and took a long, deep sniff. From that moment on, he was her puppy and she was completely tolerant of anything he did.

It's a cruel thing that dog's lives are so short compared to ours, but time was catching up with her. Her back legs barely worked, she was incontinent, sometimes in pain, and spent many hours sleeping by the stove in the kitchen.

One day when Sam was a toddler, just experimenting with bipedal motion, he started forward, lost his balance, then staggered backwards the full width of the kitchen, falling heavily on Mishi's sore hip. They say 'let sleeping dogs lie' and Mishi was instantly and painfully awoken from a deep sleep. She turned, open-mouthed, lips curled towards the source of her pain, saw it was Sam, and...... licked him on the face. Even now, almost thirty years later, there are tears in my eyes as I write this.

CHAPTER 4

RIVERS, LAKES, CANOES AND CHERT

Chris was chained to the house with two young children when the possibility to do some more extensive survey work in northern Ontario came up unexpectedly. I was asked to provide a proposal to conduct a survey of the Biscotasi and Mississagi River Provincial Parks in northern Ontario for the Ministry of Natural Resources. It was another dream project. I prepared a proposal, submitted it, then waited to hear.

I hate waiting. That phone just refused to ring. I wanted to hear that we had the job. I wanted to be able to plan, to organize, to get ready. Instead, I had to hang around twiddling my thumbs, not wanting to leave my office, but hating to stay.

I created a vivid mental picture of how it would be. The weather would be fine with little humidity. The scenery would be stunning. Our passage across and around lakes would not be troubled by irritating headwinds or excessive chop. Our campsites would be picturesque and conveniently placed exactly when we wanted to stop for the day. We would work long satisfying days and our findings would be extensive and significant. There would be no biting insects and no other people. It would be lucrative and soul satisfying.

Hanging around the house, with one ear cocked waiting for the telephone to ring, was something that my mind and body rebelled against. I found myself getting more and more tense, my stomach tied in knots, my temper short. I was virtually paralysed, unable to build up the enthusiasm or initiative to do anything constructive. My mind kept wandering back up to the Mississagi.

Instead of getting on with scraping paint off the east wall of the house, or fixing the plaster in the bedrooms, I moped about, drinking altogether too much beer and accomplishing nothing.

Eventually I got to the point where I could stand it no longer. It took nearly all my courage to do it, but I phoned Rick Hornsby at the Ministry of Natural Resources in Chapleau to ask whether they had made a decision on the Mississagi project. I had spoken to Rick on a number of occasions, and felt quite comfortable talking to him. Still, I was anxious to get a decision, and nervous as to what I might hear.

Rick couldn't provide me with the answer I sought, although he did say that he had forwarded his decision to his manager for approval. When I asked whether it was still worth my while maintaining my interest in the project, he replied in the affirmative. Be still my beating heart! As soon as I got off the phone to Rick, I called Steve to tell him the news.

I'd first met Steve while working on excavations of the 17th century French Fort Frontenac in downtown Kingston. He'd sloped onto the site, looking to see whether he could volunteer for a while. 30 years later, we're still working together. He's one of those annoying people who never forgets anything, can quote vast sections from Shakespeare and from books you've only just discovered yourself, but, he read decades ago. He writes like Oscar Wilde, learned Norwegian and Esperanto just for the heck of it, and has absolutely no interest in responsibility or a career.

By his own account, Steve used to practice invisibility. Certainly on our first meeting little about his appearance made much of an immediate impact. He is of medium height, slightish, and neat but not excessively so. He projects a kind of distracted transparency that you normally associate with someone whose brain has been addled by far too many illegal substances. And there is something of the Dorian Grey about Steve, although in his case it is not because of overt narcissism. He appears preternaturally young for his years. This is accentuated by the complete (and natural) absence of grey hair or any signs of a receding hairline.

My female friends tell me he is attractive, not so much

because of his good looks, but because of his courteousness, attentiveness, and a sort of understated masculinity. He is almost magically articulate, spicing his conversations with strange but marvellous observations drawn from his eclectic knowledge and somewhat unusual world view. He is also somewhat prone to distracting pauses as though waiting for his synapses to fire. But this is more of an idiosyncrasy of manner than a systemic problem. He can be quiet, even taciturn for long periods of time, and on first view you might assume that he lacked physical vigour. I did, and was dead wrong. He is surprisingly tough, with vast reserves of stamina.

Steve's delight in hearing of our probable success contained the additional spice of knowing that now, in all likelihood, he would be able to survive the coming winter. We arranged to meet in Kingston to go on an almighty shopping spree at our local outdoor store. High on our list of 'must buys' were comfortable, warm waterproof boots, impervious canoe packs, and a variety of little items; such as stove fuel bottles, waterproof matches, and endless quantities of irradiated food.

We'd taken a couple of short canoe trips to Algonquin Park together, so I knew he could handle his end of the canoe, could cope with a bit of discomfort, and wasn't likely to get in a tizzy if something went wrong. And just as important, I thought we might be able to stand one another's company 24 hours a day without coming to blows.

The Tale of the Dead Pike

The thunder rolled up the lake, taking thirty seconds or more to make its way from one end to the other. We tracked its progress from the door of the tent, reluctant to be forced inside by the rain, but not particularly eager to be any wetter before nightfall. If thunder can be said to be cheerful, then this was: it lacked the menace that sometimes accompanies late summer storms and was playful rather than intimidating. It seemed to be rolling around the edges of the clouds, announcing the end of the long and dreary rain which had started as soon as we had set off from the village of Biscotasing. It reminded me of Disney's image of Zeus, carelessly dropping lightning bolts from his bed in the clouds at the close of the storm scene in Fantasia. I half expected the clouds to break and a host of winged horses - the *nudinoots*, as my kids gleefully call them - to appear to the strains of Beethoven's Pastoral Symphony. No winged horses appeared but the clouds broke and drifted apart all the same. The thunder must have heralded the trailing edge of a weather system as it drifted over us, for as the light began to fade, the remaining clouds disintegrated, the rain stopped and Steve and I were able to emerge from our tent to get our lives in order.

We had driven from Kingston to Wakami Lake Provincial Park the previous day and had arrived late, tired and unsociable. Instead of going straight to the Park staff house where we had been promised accommodation, we had found the quietest part of the park, stripped the minivan of seats and gear, rolled out our sleeping bags and lain down to sleep. No more than a minute or two passed before a large Ministry truck drove slowly by, backed up, then stopped. A slim, sandy-haired young man, dressed in the standard Ministry-brown polyester, jumped out, followed by a large dog. Steve and I were both awake so I sat up and slid open the van door.

"Are you Nick Adams?" I said I was.

"I'm Scott Milne. We've got a place for you down at the staff house, if you'd prefer."

We didn't. He didn't seem put out, just a bit surprised, and seeing that we were already set for the night he didn't press the point. We agreed to meet in the morning, once we'd had a chance to get a bit of sleep.

"Were you out looking for us, or are you just doing the rounds?' I asked.

"No, I'm chasing bears. We've got a bit of a problem with them. They are attracted to the fish cleaning tables down on the beach. It's been a poor year for blueberries, so they are all over the park. We've trapped and shipped out eight so far this summer."

Scott opened the truck door.

"C'mon Bear." The big dog reluctantly detached its nose from our gear and bounded into the truck to sit bolt upright in the passenger seat.

"See you in the morning", he said, as they drove off to hunt intruders.

By mid morning we were bouncing down the narrow gravel road to Biscotasing, our stomachs full of eggs, bacon and coffee from Fern's Cafe' in Sultan. Like so many northern Ontario roads, this one was little more than a linear gravel scar on the landscape; a bulldozer cut of expediency which revealed little of the country through which we were passing.

It has long been my opinion that you could drive all over northern Ontario, and apart from some obvious sections of the Trans-Canada Highway along the Lake Superior shore, be left with the impression that the land was dull, monotonous and uninspiring. The generally low topography and the scrubby forest does not lend itself to scenic road building. Views are rare, and not particularly entrancing. Road routes have been more determined by the availability of gravel, the need to avoid bogs, and the location of the next planned clear cut, than by the natural structure and harmony of the land.

Once you are on the water everything changes. The landscape seems to unfold before you in a logical and satisfying way. The views may not be awe-inspiring, but there is a harmony, a beauty and a perfection to the subtle interplay of lakes, hills and forest. Vistas may not be grand, but they can be vast. The glimpse of bright blue water snaking for miles between islands and low hills towards the horizon can, for me at least, be an invitation to exploration and adventure, as inspiring as any light drenched mountainside or carpet of rolling hills.

There was the expected lack of charm on the Bisco road. You cross the railroad tracks a couple of times, skirt a small lake or two, then, after about an hour, the telltale signs of the settlement - the municipal dump and the track to the radio tower - appear.

Biscotasing is a small, somewhat bedraggled collection of buildings around an indentation on one of the many arms of Biscotasi Lake. Like many northern Ontario railway towns, it has the look of a community which has outlived its commercial usefulness. Unless some significant new initiative is developed one can see that in a decade or two, Biscotasing will have become yet another northern Ontario ghost town. Although a land surveyor reported the presence of a few settlers in the area in 1870, Bisco did not exist prior to the construction of the Canadian Pacific Railway. By 1880 a small settlement had sprung up to serve the needs of the crews and surveyors who were pushing the CPR line west. Bisco rapidly grew in the 1880's, as entrepreneurs responded to the various needs of the railway construction crews, and, by all accounts, became a place where earthly needs took precedence over spiritual ones.

The Hudson's Bay Company quickly took advantage of the new railway and established a post and supply depot at Bisco. Whereas prior to the railway, the interior posts at Flying Post, Mattagami, and Green Lake had been supplied either from Moosonee on James Bay, or from La Cloche on Lake Huron, henceforth they could be outfitted from the new depot at Biscotasing. Thus Bisco became a fur-trading centre, adding this to its rapidly growing economic base.

The presence of the new post also attracted native people to the area on a more permanent basis. Biscotasi Lake had always been a centre of native activity, as had all the large lakes at or near the height of land. A reference in the journal of a Hudson's Bay Company trader at Fort Mattagami refers to the presence of the 'Bishkitising Band' in the Biscotasi Lake area, suggesting that some native people were specifically identified with the area. In all probability a group or groups of extended families used the lake as a focus of their seasonal movements. But as John Pollock's archaeological surveys on the lake in the 1970's had proven, people had been living around Biscotasi Lake for thousands of years.

Early in the twentieth century Bisco became a real boom town, as logging the nearby forests became a profitable occupation. As the logging boom tailed off, and CPR began to retract, Biscotasing began its long economic decline.

The shallows surrounding the boat dock at Bisco are littered with debris. As we paddled away from shore we could make out the unmistakable shapes of pieces of clay pipe stem, sherds of late nineteenth and early twentieth century crockery and glass, beer cans, and an occasional stubbie[3] embedded in the soft surface of the bay; an archaeological record of all its years of settlement.

We were eager to leave the village behind us and wasted no time scooping artifacts from the water. Within minutes we had rounded a headland onto a main arm of the lake, leaving the village far behind. Biscotasi Lake Provincial Park southern boundary lies about five miles north of the village, on the west side of the lake.

---

3   *Short, squat beer bottle used in Canada between 1962 and 1986*

We camped on a small headland opposite the ominously named Dead Horse Island. There had been logging camps in the area during the last decades of the nineteenth century and the early part of the twentieth century and we presumed that once the horses had had the life worked out of them they were dragged to the island to rot.

Something on the western shore of the island caught our eye. We had passed it four times before our minds finally accepted what our eyes were seeing, and we paddled over for a closer look. The pike twisted and turned at the end of four feet of dull yellow nylon cord. Its desiccated body, sun-warped and blackened, hung suspended from a dead branch overhanging the lake. Getting it up there must have been quite a trick. Someone must have stood up in a boat, cast the line over the dead branch then hauled the pike high up above head height, then somehow tied off without leaving the ends dangling. Steve and I were impressed by the feat, but depressed and puzzled by its rationale. Why would some one go to all the trouble of stringing up a two-foot long pike to rot in the wind? Was this an act of mindless brutality and reckless futility - or did it have some deeper meaning? It suggested a cruel and callous attitude to the northern forest and its natural resources, the same attitude that talks of 'trash fish' and 'pan fish' without irony, the same attitude that allowed Quebec's former Premier Robert Bourassa to make memorable statements about the terrible waste of letting rivers run unharnessed to the sea[4].

The dangling fish stayed in our minds and coloured our attitude towards the other people we saw on the lake. As the thunder rolled away we emerged from our tent to enjoy the long slow descent of the evening, but found instead that our hoped-for tranquillity was spoiled by the presence of a fishing boat trolling at the mouth of the bay. With so much lake to choose from it seemed absurd that they would choose the entrance to this bay, to fish. Was there some subconscious magnetism at work that drew people together when there were so many alternatives?

Overhead a bald eagle circled patiently around the southern end

---

4   *"Quebec is a vast hydroelectric plant in the bud and everyday, millions of potential kilowatt-hours flow downstream and out to sea. What a waste!" Robert Bourassa, Power from the North (1985)*

of Dead Horse Island, all the while pursued by a shrill and bothersome herring gull. Time after time the gull flew right up to the eagle and appeared to peck, first at its back, then at its tail feathers. The eagle paid it almost no attention, except to flinch and twist from the gulls most vigorous attacks. We couldn't believe the eagle's forbearance. With its superior flying skills, it would have been so easy for it to roll over, hook the gull in its deadly claws, and drop it from the sky. But it didn't. It seemed to have closed its mind to the pestering, and carried on circling and gliding as if it were entirely alone in the sky.

Steve and I busied ourselves with preparing a fire to dry our sodden gear. After a while we heard the noise of the idling motor change pitch. We looked up to see the small boat just heading around the corner, back to Biscotasing. The fire spread throughout the small branches, sending out crackles, spits and hisses along with a strong steady heat. We had arranged our wet socks and jackets on sticks around its perimeter, and now, as the sun began to go down, we both found a comfortable place to squat and enjoy the heat.

Sitting around a campfire as the day fades is a primeval pleasure; one that has provided comfort, relaxation, and security to people just like us for thousands of years. Like those countless generations before us, we let our minds and thoughts drift with the gently curling smoke. This country is timeless. The wind will still be rustling the trees along the lake shore next year, twenty years from now, a thousand years from now.

I thought of the chert scraper that we had found at the water's edge earlier in the day. It was as fresh and crisp as when it was last held in human hands, a few hundred years, possibly even a thousand years before. I could feel the strong current of human thought running through it. Nature, wind, water, and time had not created this. Someone had deliberately brought this piece of fine, grey rock from Lake Huron, all the way up the Mississagi or Spanish River to Biscotasi Lake. Hands like mine had held it, turned it over, examined, and evaluated it, before striking a series of carefully placed blows to shape it to its current form. It had been trimmed, sharpened, and used many times before it was finally lost. I was almost certainly the first person to touch it since that day. Was this object the only legacy of that person, to whom I now felt some connection? Apart from a few modified rocks, had he disappeared completely from the world, or did his individuality live on in the transfer of his genetic material down the generations? I thought about my own family. My brother and father have been dead now for decades, and as each year passes I can recall fewer and fewer specific moments and incidents of their lives. Their physical appearance, their faces and gestures, are beginning to elude me, although I sometimes catch some fragment of them looking back at me in the mirror. With each passing year they fade a little more, but my sense of their essential being - how they were at the core of their person - remains strong. Perhaps, in some way, I am keeping them alive. Once those who truly loved them are gone and there is no one alive to retain that memory of their nature, will they disappear too? How many years will need to pass before it is as if they had never been?

I shared my thoughts with Steve, who, as it turned out, had been pursuing a similar wavelength on the other side of the fire. He told me that his Grandfather had died while he was still a young boy and although he too had an internal image, an essence, of how his Grandfather had been, he could only recall a single phrase from all the time they had spent together.

They had been working on the roof of the local school. Steve's Grandfather was up the ladder; Steve was at the bottom. His grandfather turned around, and pointing to the tool bag said,

"Pass me that hammer."

Toilet Seats and Trihedral Adzes

We had parked our van beyond the head of the lake, where the E. B. Eddy forest road crosses the Spanish River. Spanish Chutes is a frequently used point of entry for canoeists starting a trip down the Mississagi and for fishermen and hunters using the Spanish River, Abney Lake, and Ramsey Lake. We drove past a sprinkling of cans, beer bottles, and plastic trash, and backed into an area that had been hacked out of the bush for parking. The road carried on down a steep cobble slope to the river but we realized that while we may have been able to get the van down, we would have been lucky to get it back up again without four wheel drive. We had no option but to carry the boat, the motor and all our gear the last fifty yards. Rather reluctantly we had left our canoe back at Wakami Park, and borrowed the Ministry's aluminium boat and nine horse motor for this leg of the survey. Neither of us was particularly happy about it, not relishing the noise, the smell, and the disassociation from the landscape that such machinery inevitably brought. We consoled ourselves by remembering that the boat would allow us to zip around the lake much more efficiently than we could have managed in the canoe. After all, this was supposed to be work.

At Spanish Chutes, the Spanish River falls over a broad glacially-smoothed outcrop of granite. It is charming rather than spectacular, and, for me at least, much diminished by the raw cobble and mud roads, the trash, and the usual crop of dusty RV's at the epicentre of their owners' middens. I was glad to get the boat into the river, pole across the rocks into the main channel, and head down stream.

Below the chutes the river crosses a cobble field until it meets Abney Lake, where the channel broadens, and there is enough water under the hull to let the motor down all the way. Miserable driving rain had dogged our examination of Abney Lake earlier in the week and we were quite content to turn down the Spanish River and ignore it. It was drizzling as we rounded the bend into First Lake, but a light wind had sprung up and breaks in the grey sky promised a change in the weather.

First Lake is more of a marsh than a lake. Just finding enough water to keep the boat moving was a challenge. We bogged down in gyttja[5] more times than I care to remember, and had to extricate ourselves by poling and sculling our way out of the adhesive ooze. Open water did not necessarily mean deep water. Often the most navigable channel was through sparse stands of Swamp Horsetails; where they congregated densely, the water was a mere skim above the surface of the muck.

The deeper waters of Cat Bay were also rougher. A stiff wind had blown up from the southwest, throwing up a short, steep chop which smacked the prow of the boat and sprayed us both. We had discarded our rain gear with the exertions of First Lake, so we stopped briefly to make ourselves waterproof again and to put on

---

5   *Decayed vegetation, more commonly called "loon shit"*

our life vests. Steve adjusted some of the packs, so that he could hunker down in the prow below the level of the wind and spray before we set off for the south end of the lake.

Ramsey Lake is huge and sprawling, full of islands, narrow linear bays, and misleading headlands. Its water levels are controlled by a dam at its south end, which separates it rather artificially from Biscotasi Lake, and which has raised its shorelines by a few feet. This effect is really only noticeable nearest the dam, where the low shores and numerous submerged stumps betray the lake's former shape, but, as we were to discover as our survey proceeded, it has resulted in the inundation of virtually all the ancient sites around the lake's shores.

The Mississagi River Provincial Park includes only part of the southern end of the lake. Everything south of Hog Island, including the huge Southern Bay, lies to the south of the somewhat arbitrary zig-zag line across the water, which forms the parks southern boundary, a boundary drawn with little regard to the natural topography of the landscape. It had taken rather less time to reach the far end of the lake than we had anticipated, and while the chop made the journey bouncy, wet and uncomfortable, it hadn't really hindered our progress. After a brief lunch of oxtail soup on one of the low, wave-washed islands near the dam, we got started on the survey.

On our long ride down the lake we had not seen a single person. A houseboat was moored in one of the shallow bays on the west side of the lake, but since we were well off shore, we had not been able to tell whether it was inhabited. As we were beaching the boat to check out a couple of likely-looking locations, we heard the drone of an outboard. Steve finally spotted the boat, well offshore, heading away from us, flat out, towards the dam. If the three hooded and hunched figures on board had noticed us, they gave no indication as they passed.

"I wonder if that means we've got the lake to ourselves? I hope so," Steve said.

Had anyone been there to see, they would have thought we looked pretty strange. Steve took off from one side of the boat and I the other, walking slowly, heads down, peering into the shallows, and at the narrow band of wave-washed sediments along the shore. What would they think we were doing? Looking for jewellery and coins from summer bathers' pockets? Beach-combing for fishing lures?

Actually that's not far from the truth. Steve was constantly finding stranded plugs and tangled spinners in the debris along the lake shore. He seemed to have a special affinity for those complex lures with shiny spoons, plastic green and orange faceted beads, swivels and tassells. As soon as he found one he would pull the needle-nosed pliers from his canvas tool bag, snip off the treble hooks and attach it to the back of his life vest to swing and jingle with the miscellany of assorted lures and feathers he had collected.

We were looking for were tell-tale signs of past human occupation; the debris from past lives which the incessant scouring of the waves might have dragged from the nearby sand terrace. I was happily following a clear set of wolf prints when Steve shouted for me to join him. His tone provided absolutely no indication of the significance of his discovery. The Hope Diamond, a solitary chert flake, or a couple of mating Shad flies would elicit the same level of enthusiasm. You learned to take your chances.

Steve was crouched down looking at something at the very edge of the water.

"What do you make of this."

He was pointing to what, at first, looked like a fat, green segmented worm - some strange kind of fishing lure perhaps? I reached down and picked it up. Rather than squishing in my fingers, this object was hard, metallic, and obviously man-made. I laid it in my hand and we both looked it over.

"Look," I said, "It's broken here at each end, and each of these segments seems to be separate."

We looked carefully at each end. The greenish colour was missing at the ends; instead they were golden bronze and showed signs of recent breakage.

"That looks like a wire or rod going through the middle of the whole thing," Steve said. "You know what I think this is. I think these are copper beads on a wire. We should look around and see if there is anything else here."

Together we carefully searched the area. Within a few minutes we found some more beads, thirteen in all, and some long thin copper rods with points at either end - Awls. We carefully packaged the artifacts so that they would not be damaged, marked the place where we found them, and expanded our search. After scrutinizing the shore, we turned our attention to the eroding face of the sand terrace, then tested the terrace itself. Our efforts were rewarded with the discovery of a single tiny chert flake, and a spread of fire cracked rock; not enough to aid our interpretation and certainly not much to add to what we already knew.

What I already knew, or at least guessed at, subject to being able to check some reports back at home, was that these artifacts were old. Quite old. By about 5,500 years ago people in the Upper Great Lakes had discovered and begun to use copper to make a wide variety of tools, weapons, and ornaments.

Copper, in a relatively pure form, is found in nodules and lumps along the eastern coast of Lake Superior, on the Keweenaw Peninsula, on Isle Royale and in parts of Wisconsin. Native people of the region had cold hammered this raw metal into quite a variety of tools and objects of personal adornment - adzes, beads, knives, spears and occasionally votive objects. And they had peddled them widely across the Upper Great Lakes, using an extensive network of trade routes, and inter-community contacts.

The zenith of the use of copper occurred between four and five thousand years ago, at, or shortly after the time when water levels in the Upper Great Lakes were much higher than present, and when the climate in much of northern Ontario was more like that of lands further south.

A few years before, Thunder Bay archaeologists Bill Ross and Dave Arthurs had submitted three copper spear heads for radio-carbon dating, using the new accelerator technology at the University of Toronto. They were not trying to date the copper itself of course: radio- carbon dating can only be used on organic substances. Rather, they were attempting to date fragments of wood preserved by copper salts which, over time, had leached into the wooden spear shafts. The shafts had rotted away thousands of years ago, but the preserved fragments of wood were large enough to provide a date.

Bill and Dave were thrilled to get dates which indicated that the objects were from between 4,630 and 4420 years old; dates which coincided with, and confirmed their expectations. These dated objects were excavated from a large, partially-destroyed camp site on the shores of Lake Superior. But many, if not most of the copper artifacts known from archaeological sites of this period come from burials. At least, that has tended to be the case where any technical examination has occurred at the time of discovery. Unfortunately, in too many instances, the objects have been found and dug out of their surrounding in such a way that it has been impossible to derive much scientific information from the sites.

We could find no further evidence at this site to support our suspicion that the copper artifacts Steve had found on the beach had also once been buried as grave offerings. We guessed that since the lake was dammed, the rise in water levels has sped up the erosion of the sand terrace behind the beach, dragging the beads, awls, and whatever else once accompanied them, down onto the active zone along the water's edge.

That night we camped on a small island near the middle of Ramsey Lake from which we had virtually uninterrupted views up the East Arm of the lake and up Cat Bay. The low horizon, so dominant during the day, became a thin, indistinct line, framing the enormous sky as the last glimmers of light faded in the northwest. Stars began to emerge and the sky seemed to expand. It was so warm that it was like a summer night. Our tent was pitched on a thin skim of forest soil caught in a pocket in the surface of the rock - a pocket Steve had found none to his liking and from which he had set about removing rocks and roots to level it.

The rock sloped evenly from our tent toward the water, disappearing beneath the black surface to unimaginable depths. In daylight it would have been perfectly welcoming, and safe place from which to dive and swim, but as the blue of the daytime water gave way, first to murky grey, then finally to black, the playground of minnows and wavering leeches was transformed. It was all too easily to imagine survivors from the Cretaceous, lurking in the gloomy depths.

Squatting on my heels on the sloping rock, I watched the day fade. Nine thousand years had passed since the last glacial ice had ground over that rock and exposed it, as fresh and clean as an agate from a lapidary's mill. During nine thousands years, rains had washed over its surface, shore ice had ground and wrenched at it's edges, and adventurous trees had sought out it's minute fissures. Apart from some mineral and vegetation staining, a couple of streaks of aluminium from someone's fishing boat, and some cracks and fractures where camp fires had heated and shattered the rock, it was virtually unchanged.

Nine thousand years. Three million nights and days, give or take a few thousand, of sun, rain, snow, storm and calm. These had had negligible effect on that glacially smoothed surface. During those nine thousand years almost all of Ontario's human history had been written on the landscape. In this part of the world, the whole expanse of the human record, about four hundred generations in all, has taken place since these rocks last bore the burden of glacial ice. Compared to the age of the rocks themselves, all those human lives were little more than a rustle in the wind. This rock was unimaginably old.

Long before our species came into existence, before the age of mammals, before the great reptiles, even before life itself, these rocks had solidified, cooled and taken on the essential structure I could feel through my feet. The Ontario Department of Mines' report of the Geology of the Biscotasing Area defined the rocks we were camped on as Archean gneissic granite of Algoman age - not the oldest rocks in the area, but at over 2,500 million years old, they wither human conceptions of time.

In dealing with the human past on a daily basis, I have developed an ability to get my mind around hundreds, thousands, even tens of thousands of years. Trying to get a handle on geological time is another matter. Had humans begun their existence at the same time as the Algoman rocks (which, of course they didn't), about 100 million generations would by now have passed. Whole mountain ranges would have been built of our bones. It was an eerie sensation squatting there, looking out over the stillness of the lake, viscerally feeling the extreme transitory nature of my existence and even of the order of creatures to which I belong.

The camp fire Steve had constructed cast a flickering light which was soon swallowed up by the overwhelming night. From my position on the rock slope, not thirty feet from the fire, I could see him clearly, sitting on a log, carving out a spruce paddle as a present for his two year old son John. The blackness seemed deepest just around the periphery of the firelight as if the night closed in to extinguish the unwelcome light. Away from the fire, even late at night, there was always enough light to see by.

On a clear night in the bush, the number of stars visible and the intensity of their light is astounding. By day it is possible, even natural, to blunder along, focused only on ourselves and our own little world. At night the blinkers are off and we are forced to face the realization that our little blue ball of a world is a tiny, insignificant speck, circling a tiny, insignificant star, whirling in one of the countless galaxies in the vast, expanding universe. Coping with geological time scales seems child's play compared to the difficulties of grasping stellar distances and the antiquity of space.

As scientific understanding of the universe has evolved, so our world has shrunk. We used to be at it's centre; now we know we are not. Armstrong and company nailed the last spike when they beamed back pictures of our planet from the moon. Now we could all see that, like Horton's Whos, we drift in space in a universe beyond our comprehension and control. That sense of cosmic isolation can be overwhelming. For an instant my life, all human life, seemed as transitory, as meaningless and as unnoticed as those pine needles caught in the cracks in the rock beneath my feet. Yet in that same instant, and at some fundamental level, I suddenly felt precious and connected to the universe in a way I had not experienced before: no longer apart but a part of the world. It was inexplicable, sudden and profound, and has stayed with me since.

Steve had put away the paddle and was stoking the fire, sending sparks floating up in the pillar of smoke. After a while I moved back into the light and asked him the big question.

"Do you want some hot chocolate?"

We mixed our powder and boiling water, took our mugs away from the fire and stood together for a long time on that sloping rock, spotting shooting stars and satellites as they raced across the sky.

The cough of the outboard motor broke the silence of the morning. A thin mist had accumulated over the surface of the water during the night, but it parted as we raced across a kilometre of open water to another of the numerous small islands at the junction of the bays and soon disappeared as the sun rose.

As we approached both Steve and I could see something which didn't seem quite right. In a world of green and black trees, grey and reddish brown rocks, and blue sky and water those things which are not part of the natural world stand out clearly. The object we could see on the island shore seemed completely out of place - startling white against a background of yellowish brown grass. I cut the throttle and we drifted in towards the shore. Smooth granite sloped evenly down to the lake shore from a level grassed clearing.

On one side of the clearing we could see a framework of small spruce trees, still with fragments of a blue plastic tarpaulin attached to it. On the other was the mystery object - a plastic and aluminium chaise longue - a bloody lawn chair!

"I knew we forgot something." Steve said, as he tied the boat to a tree root at the shore.

"Can you imagine sitting back at home checking off your inventory of supplies and equipment. Food - check, clothes - check, beer - check, tarpaulins - check, plastic lawn chairs - check."

We scouted and tested the area finding a plethora of modern garbage strewn around the site, a brimming cesspit beneath a plastic toilet seat and a few flakes of chert in the soil pockets between the rocks. The beer cans and candy bar wrappers suggested that the most recent campers had been American. The tampon applicators and tightly rolled toilet paper packages in the cess pit indicated women, certainly more than one. Were they here alone, from choice? Or did they idle their days away reading magazines in the lawn chairs (the remaining one was broken and abandoned) drinking weak beer while their hubbies chased lunkers down the lake?

Did time weigh heavily on their hands? Were they glad to pack up their belongings, collect up a bag full of garbage, throw it in the bush and get the hell out of there? Would they ever come back? We created a myth we could live with. Coming to this little island in Ramsey Lake had not been their idea. They had indulged their husbands for a while and stuck it out. Now they were back in the suburbs of Flint or Cleveland shopping at Price Chopper and glad of it, saying 'next year the men can go on their own if they like'. We named the site in their honour.

At the bottom end of Ramsey Lake the effects of flooding had been quite obvious. The remains of flooded forests and thinly covered shoals showed that the water level was artificially raised. As we worked up the lake these effects became less noticeable, indeed we began to realist that compared to most years the lake level was down - perhaps even within a few feet of pre-dam levels.

One site brought this into perfect focus. Under normal circumstances it would have appeared as a small offshore island, separated from a larger island by a narrow stretch of shallow water. This is the way it is indicated on the topographical maps, and is certainly the way it has been since the first wooden logging dams were built on Ramsey Lake in the 1880's. We arrived to find that instead of a narrow channel, an isthmus had appeared, and where fish normally swam, and narrow neck of sand and mud was visible.

I lifted the motor and we beached the boat. Steve immediately noticed some chert flakes lying in the soft mud at the lake shore.

"Hey Nick, do you recognize this stuff?"

He picked up a handful of debitage and held it out. There were a few small thinning flakes of Hudson's Bay Lowland Chert, a couple of quartz shatter fragments, a secondary flake of jasper and some larger flakes of a translucent chert I did not recognize.

Hudson's Bay Lowland Chert is somewhat of a catchall name for a high quality chert which is found throughout northern Ontario in till deposits. It is highly various in colour ranging from dark grey, through mauve to almost cream, but whatever it's colour, it is universally waxy, lustrous and easy to work, breaking in a reliable and consistent manner. HBL, as archaeologists abbreviate it, was extensively used by native people throughout the pre-Contact past. Although strictly speaking the term should only be applied to cherts derived from Palaeozoic rocks of the Hudson's Bay Lowlands, and redeposited by the glaciers as tills throughout the north, it has been applied to just about any high quality chert from Ontario's north-land, leading to some confusion and mis-identification in the archaeological literature.

In an attempt to refine identifications Dr. Patrick Julig, of Lakehead University, subjected a number of samples from known sources to instrumental neutron activation analysis (INAA). His results suggest that archaeologists haven't done a bad job of identification in the past, although in some instances Lake Superior

Agates and Knife River Flint from North Dakota may have been misidentified as HBL.

The quartz fragments in Steve's hand were typical of what one might expect to find on pre-Contact sites throughout northern Ontario. Quartz is a silica rich mineral found in veins throughout the Canadian Shield. It is present in narrow bands of crystals on almost every exposed rock and shoreline, and as water and ice rolled pebbles on every lake shore and stream bed. Although it was freely available for tool making, it was only used in a pinch because even though it has an aesthetic appeal, it fractures unreliably and was difficult to work. For every tool made, numerous shatter fragments would have accrued.

The HBL and quartz flakes were expected. They cropped up on virtually every pre-Contact site I had ever examined in the north. The jasper and the translucent chert were more intriguing. Jasper is red chert - red from the presence of haematite, an iron ore. It is well-known in northern Ontario as those fine, blood red spots in puddingstone - that pretty rock conglomerate of polished clock faces, book ends and decorative plaques. But the jasper in puddingstone is only present as small flecks and pebbles. If we were finding flakes of the stuff on this site, it suggested that the First Nations people of the area had access to larger pieces - perhaps even a primary deposit - a vein or outcrop.

The translucent chert presented even more of a puzzle. I thought I was familiar with most of the rocks which native people had made tools from in this part of the world, yet here was a high quality, desirable chert, clearly with very acceptable working properties, that I had never seen before.

We looked at it closely. It's surface was very slightly granular, and some of the pieces had very faint streaks of red and black within them. It ranged in colour from almost quartz clear to milky or creamy grey. Was it an exotic; a desirable chert acquired in trade from somewhere far away? Or could it be local? I thought I remembered seeing artifacts made from a rock somewhat similar which had been found on archaeological sites lower down the Spanish River. Those had been tentatively identified as 'Ramah chert' from Labrador or northern Quebec - although only on the basis of a cursory visual inspection. I wondered if these could be the same.

We finished a detailed surface mapping of the site then pushed the boat back out into the lake. Were the people in this area trading with folks as far away as northern Quebec or was this chert from a local, and as yet unidentified local source? Certainly it would have been easy enough to get to a common meeting ground or to meet middlemen on James Bay. Even today it is relatively easy to paddle from Ramsey Lake into Biscotasi, cross over into the Arctic watershed at the top of Biscotasi Creek, follow the Little Rush and Opeepeesway Rivers to the Woman River and Horwood Lake.

Below Horwood Lake it is a straightforward paddle down the Groundhog River to the Moose River and James Bay. The northern bay of Biscotasi Lake still bears the name 'Flying Post Bay', marking it as the route to Flying Post, an important Northwest Company, and later Hudson's Bay Company Post on the shores of Groundhog Lake.

A more detailed examination of these cherts would have to wait until after the fieldwork. We could speculate all we wanted, and you can be sure we did, but until we could examine the rocks more closely, and get the informed opinions of others, it would be an enjoyable but meaningless game.

Once the mist had burned off we were treated to a glorious day. The wind we had been anticipating failed to appear, the lake stayed calm, and the temperature hovered in the sixties. As far as we could see, we had the lake to ourselves. We were happy.

We worked our way up the lake, checking and testing numerous areas, finding sites in some places, none in others; a typical days archaeological survey. By mid-afternoon we had reached a cluster of islands near the upper end of Cat Bay. Although we would eventually examine them all, one in particular caught our eye.

The main part of the island was shaped like a huge whale's back - steep at the front, but tailing off more gently to the rear. On one side a low, almost horizontal shelf of bedrock provided an easy boat landing and dry footing for exploring the rear of the island without climbing up hump. From the moment we landed neither of us had any doubt that we would find something here. It had the right feel - it was just a matter of time.

Can a place retain the resonance of the people who have been there before? Can we be receptive to such resonances if they exist? Such things are probably not measurable in ways acceptable to science. I know though, that on occasions too numerous to be coincidence, I have been drawn to a particular spot, knowing that evidence of past lives awaited discovery.

Whether I have been responding to a subtle collection of visual clues that I have been unable to identify, or whether the human mind, once open to such influences, is capable of tuning in to echoes of other lives, I don't know. I do know though, that the feeling is almost never wrong.

Steve lay his pack on the flat granite, took off his jingling life vest, and went to examine the water's edge along the island's west shore. I hopped from rock to rock, peering into the water near to where we had landed the boat. On my third rock, I stopped short. Below, in about nine inches of water, two objects had caught my eye. The first of these was a palm-sized piece of milky grey chert. Even through the water I could see that the long edge of the flake had been trimmed and straightened to form a sharp cutting edge. Nearby I could see a long, narrow rock, broad at one end, slightly narrower at the other. It looked like nothing more than a long, narrow rock, but in the course of my work in northern Ontario I had seen other such rocks, that on closer inspection had turned out to be rather more interesting. I bent down and pulled them, in turn, from the shallow pool.

It was a beautiful, large, flake tool: its cutting edge still crisp and keen, and it was made of that same translucent chert we had noticed further down the lake. But this tool was made from a primary flake - one of the big flakes driven off during the initial preparation of a block or large cobble. As a tool it was nice enough, but it hardly seemed likely that such an unrefined object could have travelled far. Normally only completed or near complete objects were traded over long distances. Could this chert be from a local source after all?

I must have made some peculiar noises when I had first seen the artifacts in the water, because by the time I pulled the second object clear of the surface, Steve was standing next to me. I handed him the large flake knife to look at while I examined the rock. It was about a foot long, four inches wide at the fat end then tapering back to about two inches wide at the narrow end. It looked a bit like a fin-less whale shark with backache; wide and thin at the front, humped in the middle then tapering off towards the tail. I turned it over. Yes! The underside of the 'whale shark's' mouth had been ground even and smooth across its whole width - trihedral adze.

Although not common anywhere, trihedral adzes have been found in a number of places across northern Ontario. Regrettably few are known from what archaeologists call 'good contexts', meaning found in circumstances where they were in or near materials which could be dated by scientific means. Archaeologist Bill Fox's 1980 study of trihedral adzes from a number of sources led him to conclude that they dated to the early part of the Shield Archaic; that is, to between 6,000 and 8,000 years ago. At that time, the climate in northern Ontario was marginally warmer than it is today, white pines dominated the landscape, and people appear to have needed large, heavy cutting tools. Bill concluded his article by saying,

"...considering the above data, it is proposed that the trihedral adze, and perhaps the entire ground biface industry in Northwestern Ontario, is of an early Shield Archaic provenance, dating to between 4,000 and 6,000 B.C. That these dates bracket the white pine maximum in the area may not be fortuitous, and could indicate that local Native bands had adjusted their tool repertoire in order to utilize these large conifers".

In his circumspect way, and reading between the lines, Bill is implying that trihedral adzes were probably used to cut down and hollow out those great big trees to make dug-out canoes.

As we left Cat Bay and swung into the shallows of First Lake we were still struggling with some weighty problems. Were the adze and the large flake contemporary, or was it a mere accident of fate that they were together in the same pool? Could there be a local source of jasper that people were tapping into? Was there some chronological or physical relationship between the jasper and the translucent chert? Could we make it back to Fern's in Sultan for a triple decker and beer before they closed?

We poled, motored, paddled, sculled, cursed, and sweated our way back through the Holocene ooze. At midpoint we passed a group of men, setting up two large pole and tarp shelters on the edge of the marsh, presumably getting ready for the annual moose slaughter. The beer was already unloaded and the serious work of emptying the bottles had begun. Steve scanned the scene for lawn chairs, but there were none visible. They were probably still in the boats. The men must have sensed our antipathy, and barely a hand was raised or head nodded as we struggled passed. Maybe they had thought they had the lake to themselves.

On the Mississagi River

The bear's head gently swayed in the wind, twenty feet from the ground and was beginning to attract a crowd of flies. Rick had shot it a couple of days earlier when, after repeated warnings, trappings and relocations, it had continued to plague the fishermen at Wakami Park wharf. That, in itself, was not a capital crime. Numerous bears were attracted to area, the allure of fish guts proving more irresistible than the scant harvest of blueberries in the surrounding forests. As Rick had explained to us, they trapped quite a few each year, trucked them to a variety of locations forty or fifty miles away, and let them go. They always sprayed their coats with a patch of indelible paint so that they could recognize them again. This particular bear, however, had proven singularly persistent and aggressive. It hadn't liked moving on when given a polite tap on the rear with a shovel, and had become a real problem.

After its execution, the bear had been skinned, butchered and decapitated. The meat was in the ministry freezer and the head had been hung out to be picked clean by birds and insects so that the skull could be used in the Park's interpretive programs. Now it hung out of reach, close to the ministry's workshop where we had gathered to fix the shock absorbers on the van.

We had been having trouble ever since our first trip to Bisco the previous week. The rough, cobble and gravel roads, were proving too much for the weakly-sprung minivan, which seemed content to shed shock absorbers at the first opportunity. On our way back down south the previous week a hanger bolt had sheared, nearly throwing us off the road when we po-goed over some washboard on the highway. We had limped into Sudbury and replaced both the shock absorber and the bolt - now it had done it again. Rick opened up the workshop and we sorted out tools and an appropriate bolt from the array of equipment. This time it didn't take too long, and by mid-afternoon we were on our way to Spanish Chutes.

Our journey to Spanish Chutes gave Rick a chance to get to know us a little better, and us him. He seemed intrigued by Steve - particularly in his military career and how that related, if at all, to our current work. Rick proudly admitted to having spent many years in the Army Cadets, enjoying the discipline, the hard work, and the structure. He had seriously entertained the idea of going to Royal Military College in Kingston, but had finally opted for th University of Guelph instead.

The absence of military training in my life came as no great surprise to him - although he seemed a trifle disconcerted when I mentioned that my four-week stint of paramilitary training at Outward Bound School in the late sixties had been enough to put me off it for life. I'm not sure Rick could reconcile the obvious differences in Steve's backgrounds and mine, with our quite evident capacity to get along well together.

Steve is a constant source of surprise to me, and I could see he was also beginning to puzzle Rick. His mild, diffident manner and his obvious intellectual strength seem incompatible with military life. He seems more like an ageing flower child than a former infantryman. On first meeting, and even on second, fifth of fifteenth, you would think that the idea of being in close company with hoards of other men with whom he had little in common would be anathema. Yet as I listened to them talk, I was once again reminded of Steve's great fondness for the time he spent in the services. He positively enjoyed the training, the manoeuvres and the travel. Indeed, the only times about which I have ever heard him complain, are those when he was cold - something I found easy to understand, since he still becomes torpid and intractable when the temperature dips.

After this most recent fix, the van was behaving itself, and it did not take too long to get to Spanish Chutes. Rick helped us unload our gear and haul it down to the water's edge while I pulled the canoe off the roof. The combination of digging gear, camping equipment, clothes, supplies, and food for 20 days, made for a fully loaded canoe, but I was pleased to see that we still had plenty of free-board once we pushed off from the shore. We had arranged that Rick or Scott would drive the van down to the bottom end of the park, on Rocky Island Lake, and leave it there. Once we completed this leg of the trip we would be able to pick up the van and head back to Chapleau without delays. It seemed like a good idea at the time.

As we pushed off from shore, we glanced over our shoulders in time to see that Rick had turned the van around and was heading back up the road to Sultan. A breeze was gusting down the river towards us, rustling the willows along the banks, and pushing against us with the current. We were so pleased to be moving again that we hardly noticed.

We paddled barely a mile of wide, shallow river before the banks had closed in where the river flows over a narrow, rock-strewn boulder field. Under high water conditions we may have been able to line the canoe up this swift, but since water levels were low, we had no option but to head for the portage sign on the left bank. The portage skirted the low ground next to the swift and ended up at a rock-strewn landing at the head of the rapids. Even though it was still quite early, we opted to camp at the head of the swift instead of heading off into Spanish Lake. Our testing around the portage would take quite some time, we had noticed a rather attractive camp site on a bedrock knoll just in from the end of the portage, and the stiff breeze disinclined us from proceeding further.

As time wore on, we slowly made progress down river, searching and testing as we went. Sometimes the weather was foul, sometimes glorious. We were constantly in and out of the canoe, checking, testing and moving on, using all the available daylight for work and only stopping for a few minutes around lunch time, for a mouthful of crackers and cheese. Sometimes the biting insects were brutal, sometimes benign. Each day we had to pitch camp, prepare food, clean up, sleep, eat breakfast, break camp, move on. It was a tiring, but very satisfying and enjoyable routine.

From Bardney Lake, a long portage leads to Sulphur Lake, then across the height of land between the Spanish River and the Mississagi River drainages into Surprise Lake, which is not much more than a big, swampy pond. We camped at the end of the portage amid low alder bushes alive with migrating warblers.

You might think that after paddling and working all day we would have had enough, but once we'd eaten some supper, and as the light was fading, we slid the empty canoe into the water for a quiet spin around the lake. We had been seeing bald eagles and ravens virtually every day and here was no exception. The raven's musical gurgling and deep croaking rang out across the still water. Back at the campsite while I started to get a fire going for the mandatory hot chocolate, Steve grabbed a shovel and screen and astonished me by saying,

"I think I'll just dig a few more holes."

At over one kilometre, the portage over to Circle Lake is the longest on the whole route. It doesn't sound like much when you write it down but when you've canoe, paddles, packs, shovels, screens, and camping gear to haul, it's a long way. We had our routine well-organized by now. Steve grabbed his pack, slung the food pack on top, grabbed whatever he could carry in his hands, and set off walking. I slid the paddles under the canoe thwarts, hoisted it onto my shoulders, and set off behind him. Portaging is an exercise in pain management. At first the canoe feels light and easy to carry, but as the distance increases the pressure of the thwart on your shoulders starts to intrude. By the half way point mine were screaming, so I left the canoe propped against a fallen tree and returned for the rest of the gear. Steve had carried on right to the end.

The walk back is always a relief. Freed from the weight, your legs feel strong and ready for anything. I collected the remaining pack and gear, then set off back along the path. In the meantime, Steve had dumped his burden at the end of the portage and was returning to the mid point.

When we had both made it back to the canoe, we took a little break. There's something very pleasant about sitting in the middle of completely undisturbed, natural jack-pine forest, listening to the wind in the tree tops and the occasional rustling of a mouse or a small bird in the pine needles on the forest floor, knowing that at that moment, you are many miles from the nearest people and completely reliant on your own resources. Steve chose that moment to inform me that there was very fresh bear scat at the far end of the portage, so we'd better keep our eyes open.

Close to the end of the portage, there is a steep downward section with loose gravel under foot. Stepping down one of the steeper parts, my leading foot slipped, the tail of the canoe bashed the ground behind me and I sank to my knees, with one leg forward and one back. For a few seconds I wasn't sure whether I had damaged myself, but fortunately it was just a slip – I was soon ready to continue.

Despite the bear shit all around us, we had lunch sitting on a log, looking out onto the end of Mississagi Lake. This was the head of the Mississagi River; from here, the paddling would all be down hill.

We used an old logging camp on Mississagi Lake as our base for the next couple of days while we explored and tested, in the process finding archaeological evidence spanning many thousands of years. At one site we found a French gun flint and a small, white, oval trade bead which archaeologist Ian Kenyon, an acknowledged expert in such things, subsequently identified as being from the 'Champlain Period' and dating to about 1615. The people travelling on Mississagi Lake almost certainly acquired these items from their neighbours along the north shore of Lake Huron, who, in turn, probably acquired them from French traders in Huronia or along the St. Lawrence River.

Eventually, we moved down river to Upper Green Lake. The wind was rising steadily, and by the time we reached the lake, its surface was choppy, and we had a hard time making our way along the shore to Mississagi Lodge, the only structure of any permanence along the whole canoe route.

In our background research we had come across conflicting information that the lodge may, or may not have been built on the site of a Hudson's Bay Company Post. Since it also occupied the most attractive and logical place for First Nations settlement, we had to check it out. There were boats pulled up on shore and smoke rising from the chimney so there were obviously people around. We knocked on the door.

What follows has to be understood in the knowledge that neither Steve nor I are the most sociable of people, but the door opened, and before we had a chance to introduce ourselves, a big elderly man with a strong mid-western accent hustled us inside.

"Hello Guys – would you like ham and potatoes? I imagine you're hungry. Sit yourselves down right here. Jim, get these guys some food on their plates. Would you like some coffee? I'm Dick, and you are......?"

We introduced ourselves, and between gulps of coffee and mouthfuls of food, we explained why we were there and what we were doing. There were five or six men, all late middle age, all American, and Dick was clearly leader and spokesman. He explained that they regularly came up to the lodge to fish and were used to taking in canoeists.

Upper Green Lake isn't particularly large – only about three miles long and one mile wide, but it has a reputation for throwing up on-shore waves which often prevented canoeists from passing by. I think Dick and his friends rather enjoyed the opportunity to be hospitable, and meeting the paddlers on the river, helped break the monotony of fishing, cooking and cleaning which is the inevitable pattern of camp life.

As we ate and chatted, the wind continued to blow. After lunch, Steve and I tested around the buildings and along the narrow sand spit between the lake and the river, finding surprisingly little evidence of First Nations camp sites, and nothing conclusive to suggest that a Hudson's Bay Post had ever been there. By the time we were ready to move on, the on-shore waves were dangerously high. Launching in to them would have been virtually impossible.

"I really don't think you should leave just yet," Dick said. "We have spare bunks, hot water, and plenty of food. You're welcome to stay until the weather changes."

On the third day, Steve and I thought it was time we left. We'd exhausted our supply of canoeing and archaeology stories, we'd tested all the sections of lake shore within walking distance, and we'd heard a lot about life in Dick's world, which seemed to include the ear of the President and many people in Congress. The other guys were an interesting mix of employees and friends and it was from Jim that we heard that Dick ran a large communications business. Jim was only a lowly dairy farmer with hundreds of acres of prime Ohio Valley bottom land.

Their hospitality and friendship were impeccable. We agreed to disagree on many topics, including politics, religion, health care, guns – the normal suite of opinions which separate Canadians from Americans – but I think we all enjoyed the conversation-wrestling which helped pass the time.

Unfortunately, the waves were just as vigorous the third day as when we arrived – but both Steve and I had agreed it was time for us to leave, despite their assurances that we were welcome to stay and their anxiety that we were about to be stupid.

Everyone came down to the shore to watch us leave. The waves were running from the south-west, while we needed to be heading south-east. Before we slid the canoe into the water I said,

"Let's head straight in to the waves until we're almost across the lake. Then we'll spin around and angle down the lake with the waves behind us".

We both knew this would be a tricky manoeuvre; if we got it right, great, but if we got it wrong, we would be in the drink.

As soon as the canoe was in the water, we knelt as low and wide as we could and paddled hard. It was a battle to keep the prow into the waves and make any headway, but eventually we were past the worst of the breaking waves and into the rollers. We couldn't relax. Despite aching arms, we had to keep forcing the canoe into the wind and waves until the far shore was only a couple of hundred yards away.

"Steve – let's spin on the crest of this next wave. Ready? Go!"

As the wave rolled under us, we dug with the paddles, turned the canoe almost completely around, and started to paddle hard downwind. Out of the corner of my eye, I could see our hosts watching from the shore, but we were too busy steering to wave. Gradually, we were able to angle slightly across the waves and head for the river exit and the portage to Kashbogama Lake. Steve managed to lift his paddle in salute, just before we left the bay and were out of sight.

A year later we were back on the same lake to finish the work. This time though, we had entered the river system from the south. As we rounded the corner we could see the full expanse of the lake and a small fishing boat sitting motionless, a couple of hundred yards out from the lodge. We continued to paddle in its direction, and as we got closer, we heard one of the fishermen say: (and here you have to remember that this is pretty much the middle of nowhere and imagine the disbelief in his voice),

"Why look Jim, it's them same two guys".

Below Upper Green Lake, the river passes through a series of smaller, many-armed lakes, each of which had to be carefully examined and tested. We entered every bay, adding many miles to the route most paddlers would take, in the process finding and documenting numerous ancient archaeological sites.

A few of the lakes had small, generally scruffy, plywood cabins built for for fly-in fishermen. Sadly, these had often be built on the most attractive camping areas, now made ugly by bare eroded ground, discarded junk and, often as not, piles of garbage.

From the water, we could see that at one of the cabins, garbage had been thrown into a shed and just forgotten. Not surprisingly, attracted by the delicious odour, a bear had torn the door off and strewn the contents around in his search for something edible. Nevertheless, it was too likely that the location had also been favoured in the distant past. We coasted gently towards the shore.

Just as Steve's end was approaching the bank, I stepped out of the canoe into about three feet of water. As we'd been gliding in, I'd seen a large piece of pre-Contact pottery in the clear water, and knew unless I got it right then, we'd never find it again. It's a good job Steve is fairly level-headed, as his end of the canoe dipped unexpectedly as my weight left the rear. I grabbed the pottery and waded to shore.

It was worth the dip. The sherd was a large piece from the rim of an early 14th century "Juntunen Ware" pot. Juntunen Ware is most common on sites in the Straits of Mackinac region of Michigan, although similar sherds are occasionally found on sites across the Lake Huron and Lake Superior shores. I'd first seen Juntunen Ware on the Whitefish Island site in Sault Ste Marie, but was quite surprised to see it this far inland, and this far north.

One of the interesting characteristics of these vessels is that they share some design elements with Iroquoian pots more typically found south of the Great Lakes. It is one of the many hints that well before the arrival of Europeans, people and ideas travelled widely throughout the region – even into the more remote corners of the 'wilderness'.

Pottery that has been sitting in water for an age is likely to disintegrate if allowed to dry out too quickly. Steve dug through his pack, found one of our cooking pots with a tight filling lid, placed the sherd in a self-sealing sandwich bag filled with water from the lake, placed that inside another sealed bag, put that in the pot then sealed it with duct tape. We would keep it in as near to its original environment for the rest of the survey, then deal with it properly when we got home. One cooking pot was a small sacrifice for such an informative find.

The last parts of the survey were conducted in October. I had replaced the inadequate minivan with a much more robust 4wd diesel truck, which served us well.

It was a wonderful time to be on the river, as long as the weather wasn't too vicious. At one campsite by a rapids, I had drunk too much hot chocolate and awoke in the middle of the night with a pressing urge to relieve myself, despite the chill in the air and my desire to stay tucked in my sleeping bag. I struggled free of the tent to the most phenomenal display of stars I have ever seen. The air was so clear, and with no light pollution to diminish them, the stars seemed only just out of reach above my head. I stood looking in amazement at the night sky, and listening to the constantly changing song of the river, until my naked skin could bear the cold no longer.

The lower part of the park is all river - the myriad of lakes have been left behind. Flowing out of Bark Lake, the river turns through a series of doglegs - old fault lines in the ancient rock landscape. In the early 20th century, the Mississagi Forest Rangers had a headquarters there from which the rangers would head out into the forest to check on fires and the activities of trappers and prospectors. Archie Belaney (Grey Owl) was one of them: his signature is reputedly carved into one of the beams on the inside of the one remaining log building from the period.

As we worked our leisurely way down the river, we came across campsites that many others had used. The places which were accessible by boat were almost always a mess: broken bottles, burned cans, unburied toilet paper, broken fishing rods, broken lawn chairs. The places only reachable by canoe were always virtually spotless.

We were a few days behind one pair of canoeists who not only had left their campsites tidy, they had carefully gathered and piled fresh, dry firewood and left it neatly next to the fire pit for the next people along. It was a simple act, repeated at each of their camps; one that hinted at their reverence for the landscape and their pleasure of being in that environment.

Rivers like this offer remarkably few places to pitch a tent. Rather like modern arterial highways, where just about everyone stops for breaks at the same gas station / coffee shop / rest area, so people travelling on the river were funnelled into the same few locations. The lands adjacent to the river are either low and swampy, or steep and rocky.

We tested all the suitable spots, paying particular attention to the portages around Split Rock and Hellgate Rapids. The former is easily runnable under the right conditions, the latter is a meat grinder which it would not be wise to try to run.

Eventually, after about twenty kilometres of rugged terrain and rapids, the river broadens into a wide swampy valley of alder, willow, and reeds with numerous oxbows and old channels. There may be a few ancient campsites along this stretch of river, but one could spend a lifetime looking. We didn't. We continued through the moose swamp towards Rocky Island Lake and the end of our survey.

Our return journey to eastern Ontario was relatively uneventful. Gone were the days of broken shock absorbers, and bottoming out at every corner. Although plenty bouncy on its heavy duty springs, the new truck just clattered along with satisfying regularity and confidence-inspiring solidity.

We had started our homeward journey well before sunrise and had reached the corner of the Sultan Road and Highway 144 while it was still dark. Nothing was moving on the roads as we roared through the silent landscape in our cocoon of warmth and mechanical noise. The darkness gradually gave way to light as we passed the signs to Halfway Lake Provincial Park and headed south towards Cartier. The mist hung on the trees and gently swirled across the surface of the many small lakes and ponds beside the road.

As we breasted the top of a hill, Steve and I saw two small shapes on the road ahead. I slowed the truck to a crawl. We edged closer in the half light, until we could make out the flurry of movement before us. A snowshoe hare was racing straight down the middle of the highway, not looking behind it, nor varying its path to left or right. Behind it, neither gaining nor loosing ground, but following with dogged intensity was a small, reddish brown creature with erect rounded ears which Steve and I immediately identified as a pine marten. We slowed the truck until we were stationed about thirty yards behind the marten. It did not appeared to notice or care about our presence. The hare was built for speed, not for distance. He lolloped along, occasionally throwing in a burst of speed when he sensed that his pursuer was closing in.

The marten was a model of consistency. His feet were a flurry of action, his path was direct, he never took his eyes off his intended prey. Even as we watched we could see that, as far as the marten was concerned, the hare was already dead. Nothing and nobody, not even a noisy diesel truck, (following at a respectful distance) was going to deter him from his breakfast. After a couple of hundred yards the hare appeared to slow, as if conceding the victory, but as the marten sprinted for the kill, the hare suddenly surged ahead with a new spurt of energy. Undaunted, the marten continued its pursuit, never relenting, never slowing, always focused on the final outcome.

Eventually the hare began to slow again and edged off towards the side of the road. Again the marten increased his speed to close the distance, but as he lunged for the kill, the hare leapt into the air, landed three feet away and blazed up the road towards the truck. When he lunged the marten had lost his footing and slithered sideways before regaining his feet, but sensing the nearing victory, he was instantly in pursuit again. As we witnessed the hare's near fatal move we had brought the truck to a complete stop, although the idling diesel still broke the misty silence of the forest.

If animals can be said to have expressions, these two wore their feelings plainly on the surface of their features. As the two animals passed within two feet of the truck, we felt we could read the vastly different feelings they were experiencing. The hare was desperate and terrified. It seemed to be running on pure instinct, having exhausted its physical reserves some time earlier. Its progress was now faltering and erratic as if it were giving up.

The marten, on the other hand, was all business. Its little furry feet must have been burning after such a long run on the hard tarmac, and its lungs must have been close to bursting. You would never know it from the look on its face. As it passed the truck, its eyes were riveted on the rear of the hare. With its erect ears it formed a perfect picture of concentration. It didn't even glance at us. As spectators we were excluded from the central drama.

As we turned around in our seats to follow their progress, we heard the sound of a vehicle approaching from the south. The animals must have heard it too, for as its lights became visible, the hare veered off into the bush at the side of the road, closely followed by the marten. I put the truck into drive and picked up speed. As we drove away I know both of us were pondering the final outcome of the chase. We felt sorry for the hare, knowing that by now it was probably kicking out its last breaths in the underbrush, the marten's teeth clamped onto its dew-soaked neck. But we also felt glad for the marten, whose determination and vigour we assumed had been rewarded in the end. We felt extremely lucky to have been able to watch even a segment of the kind of drama that must be played out thousands of times a day in the northern forests. We did not interfere, and I don't believe that we altered the outcome by our presence.

The Woman River

By the time we had finished all parts of the survey, we had discovered forty-seven previously-unrecorded archaeological sites dating from the Early Archaic period, through to the fur trade and logging eras. It was a mighty task to write the report which took most of the following winter. As I worked on the report, I thought about the chert and jasper from the headwaters lakes, plucking up the courage to apply to the Ontario Heritage Foundation for a small research grant to look for the source, and acquire some samples for comparative analysis.

The following spring I was back in the region again. Steve and his wife had moved up to the Arctic community of Puvirnituq to teach, but his brother-in-law Phil, who had worked with me on other projects was available. Chris was still tied down with the kids.

Over the winter I had spent some time reading geological reports from the general area and had decided that the most likely (or at least, a very possible) source of our mystery chert was the 'Woman River Iron Range'. This fourteen-mile long area lies between the community of Sultan and Horwood Lake not too far from the town of Chapleau. From Ramsey and Biscotasi Lakes, where we had first noticed the distinctive chert, north to the Iron Range, was just a skip and a jump. By canoeing to the north end of Biscotasi Lake, and up Biscotasi Creek, a short portage over the height of land, then north down the Little Rush and Opeepeesway Rivers, one could be at the Iron Range within two or three days paddle. The route was well-known and well-used during the fur frade era, and undoubtedly was regularly used long before that.

During the time Steve and I had been working in the area, we occasionally got groceries in Chapleau which, like many northern Ontario towns, is a bit grim and down-at-heel. We uncharitably decided it was the armpit of Ontario. Sultan, a tiny, shabby and isolated hamlet where we often ate, we decided (quite unfairly, I'm sure), it was the bubo on the armpit.

Bubo or not, Sultan was our starting point. Through studying the topographical maps, we had worked out that the easiest way to get where we wanted to be was to follow the Wakami River north from Sultan, then join the Woman River further downstream. Calling it the Wakami 'River' is a bit of a joke – it's really more of a stream which winds a tangled path through forest, swamp, and bog, every so often surprising you with a short stretch of rocky rapids or with a peaceful section through small lakes. It is classic boreal forest canoeing of the kind I like best. You never know what you will see around the next bend: an eagle, a moose, a brace of otters, or a log jam across the whole stream. There's enough scenic variety to keep you on your toes.

The trip from Wakami Lake Provincial Park, through Sultan, then downstream to Horwood Lake, used to be an official Ministry of Natural Resources canoe route. For decades, the MNR published a clear guide and maintained the portages. All this has gone by the wayside now, as government departments have reduced services, and generally stopped doing many of the useful and valuable things they once did. I'm sure some might argue that the abandonment of almost all the provinces canoe routes reflects declining interest in wilderness travel. I suspect declining wilderness travel has also been affected by government policy. Commercial interests now monopolize the landscape, ancient portages which were in use for countless generations and a critical part of northern Ontario's cultural landscape, have become overgrown. We live in a time when doing anything interesting or challenging is regarded as dangerous.

In reading the few recent canoe trip reports on the internet, I have read that local tourism operators have taken to erecting bear feeding stations right on the old portage routes. Imagine working your tired way along a portage which avoids an unnavigable rapid, stepping over fallen logs and forcing your way through grown-in vegetation, only to come across a barrel of stinking fish guts and sundry kitchen scraps, presided over by a none-to-friendly bear.

It's bad enough that this kind of bait-hunting is allowed. Over a period of weeks, poor old Bruin is trained to turn up regularly to gorge on the lovely offerings, only to be plugged by some fat-bellied cretin sitting in a tree stand above.

If the bear had any expression on his face when he died, it would have been one of astonishment, yet, dollars to doughnuts, once he's been skinned and mounted, his teeth will be bared, and his paw will be raised as if he's about to attack the poor Schlitz-drinking morons around him in the basement recreation-room.

But I digress. It was getting late in the year when Phil and I set off from Sultan, and the last thing on my mind was tubs of offal and surprised bears. We had about three days of paddling before we reached the junction with the Woman River; paddling through restful, peaceful country, broken only by the peeping of migratory birds in the bushes and the occasional, distant sound of logging equipment working somewhere, miles away.

Phil was an excellent partner: tireless, skilful, and comfortable in this environment. It's not everyone's cup of tea to be in the bush, miles from anywhere, entirely dependent on the few resources you have with you, but it didn't seem to bother him.

The Woman River Iron Range crosses the Woman River just where the Opeepeesway River joins from the south. We noted a few small archaeological sites as we travelled, but other than recording their locations so we could register the sites later, we did not tarry to test or explore further. We were hoping to find some outcrops of chert or jasper from which we could extract some samples for comparative testing with some of the artifacts Steve and I had recovered during our survey of the Mississagi River.

I had been in contact with a geologist at the Ontario Geological Survey who had kindly sent me some samples of drill cores from the Woman River Iron Range. In addition to these, Phil and I retrieved some drill core fragments from an abandoned Falconbridge mining camp at the side of the river, and bashed some fragments from various cherty outcrops, found by hiking inland on a compass bearing along the line of the Iron deposit.

When we first arrived at the abandoned mining camp, we had been thinking of camping on the flat terrace and using it as our base of exploration, but we quickly abandoned that idea. As soon as we stepped ashore, we could see that the whole area was liberally spotted with great dollops of fresh bear poop. There was so much of the stuff, we wondered whether they'd been having a picnic or some some kind of convention. We hastily gathered some samples from the broken and spilled drill core trays, and paddled away.

Curiously, a few years later, I was on the river again – this time for pleasure with my old friend Dave from New Mexico, whom I had first met while living in Spong Farm. We had been paddling in a hard, steady rain for hours when we rounded the bend near the old mining camp. However, instead of endless bear poop, the terrace was busy with exploration tents, drilling machinery and neatly-stacked, fresh drill core trays. As we paddled past, a man emerged from one of the tents and called us over to shelter for a while. While we ate their food and drank their coffee in the dry, Lloyd (I'll call him that - I have no idea what his real name was) told us that he viewed the indignity of camp life as a necessary evil part of his job as a mining geologist. He just couldn't get his head around the idea that we would be sloshing down the river and camping on wet, stony ground for the fun of it. He wanted to be home, or back in his centrally-heated office. He was not enjoying camp life at all.

As the rain continued to bucket down, Lloyd arranged bunk space for us in one of the heated tents, plied us with food, and pumped us for stories of our lives. He must have been really bored, if we were the best entertainment going.

I can no longer remember how our truck magically got to the parking area at the northern end of Horwood Lake. I suspect one of the kind folks at Wakami Lake Provincial Park must have driven it there for us. Fortunately, it was there when we arrived, so we loaded the canoe and gear and headed straight for Chapleau and the first greasy hamburger we could find.

Back at home, I had arranged through the geology department at Queen's University, Kingston, to subject the samples to INAA (Instrumental Neutron Activation Analysis) at the Slowpoke-2 facility at Royal Military College of Canada. Each sample was crushed, then exposed to the nuclear reactor for one minute in order to detect the various minerals and their percentages in each sample. By comparing the archaeological samples with those from drill cores known to have come from the Woman River Iron Range, we hoped to demonstrate that they were from the same source.

Well, things don't always go as planned. We got plenty of data from the INAA testing, but at the statistic level, the results were inconclusive.

I am convinced that somewhere along the Iron Range strike, there will be a place where First Nations people quarried translucent chert and blood coloured jasper from which to make their tools. We just haven't found it yet.

One of these days I'm going to load up the canoe again, head north up Biscotasi Lake and follow the ancient canoe route over the height-of-land and down the Woman River and seek it out.

CHAPTER 5

IT'S A LIVING

There is a tendency among archaeologists to present their work as if everything went according to plan, they had anticipated every element of the project and their excavation techniques and interpretations were flawless. The reality is that unexpected things happen, important things are overlooked, sometimes the digging is a bit shoddy, things get lost, mistakes are made and any deficiencies are cunningly concealed in the report.

For instance, it's not always easy to lay out excavation areas with any degree of precision when you are working on sloping ground, around large rocks and trees, and you are far from any fixed points of reference. This is easier now with super-accurate GPS units and total station surveying equipment, but back in the days of Dumpy levels and hand tapes, it was quite a different matter. Nevertheless, you will never find an excavation report where the excavation areas don't align perfectly with the grid or the units were precisely dug to their limits. We may be stumble-bums in the field, but we're always perfect on paper.

I only bring this up because I have made my share of mistakes over the years and I'm about to tell you – with no great enthusiasm or pride – about a big one.

My little company had been hired to conduct an archaeological survey for an expansion of the Trans-Canada Highway near Thunder Bay. Most of the work was boring and repetitious –

digging shovel test pits at regular intervals along the areas where expansion of the highway was planned, and sifting the dirt looking for artifacts. When you've done enough of this kind of survey and testing, it becomes second nature; dig, sift, look, refill, move on. To avoid hotel bills, our small crew was staying at the municipal camp ground at Trowbridge Falls. It was a delightful spot which, as the name suggests, is built around the rapids and falls of the Current River. Each night after work, we would cook up some food, sit around relaxing, then head for bed.

On the third night, we awoke to a horrible bashing and thrashing. A skunk had managed to get himself in to one of our food coolers and the lid had shut on him. Rob was the hero who somehow managed to tip the cooler and extract the skunk without getting sprayed. I imagine the enclosed space dissuaded it from letting go with a full blast, although he certainly left a bit of an aroma behind (the skunk, that is, not Rob!).

Towards the end of the survey we were working at the city end of the project when we started to find flakes in our test pits. This was neither unexpected or unusual. Thunder Bay is surrounded by a series of terraces which ring Lake Superior like scum on the sides of a bathtub. As you drive from down-town out towards the Trans-Canada Highway, you climb up a series of ridges, each one marking an ancient shoreline. It's not that the water was that high of course, but during the last ice age, the weight of up to a kilometre of ice had depressed the earth's crust. Imagine carefully pressing down on a custard or gravy skin with your finger. Just like that. Once the massive weight of glacial ice melted, the land started to rise, (just as if you'd removed your finger from the custard) pushing the old shorelines further and higher from the current lake shore. Where we were working was where the shoreline stood over 9,000 years ago. People were living along that shore, and they left plenty of evidence of their activity.

Over the years many places have been found where these early inhabitants of Ontario were living. The sites are mainly known because the people were quarrying a local rock called jasper taconite – a lovely, deep reddish purple silica rich rock – from which to make a wide range of tools including some exquisite spear points.

As always happens when we started to find artifacts, we expanded our testing grid in an attempt to gauge the extent of the site and find its boundaries. We found flakes in only 5 test pits, all the others were empty. The site seemed limited to a very small peninsula extending into what, at the time, may have been a shallow or swampy bay. I had decided that it must have been a very small camp site indeed – perhaps even somewhere where one person sat down for an hour or two and whacked out a couple of tools. This is where I made my first mistake.

Instead of recommending that the site should be subject to 'Stage 3' testing (digging a bunch of 1 metre squares on a 5 metre grid to get a better picture of the site), thinking I knew best, I recommended that we go straight to full excavation. The proposed budget was correspondingly small.

When we returned the following June to start the excavation, it didn't take long to realist my mistake. We accurately laid out the grid (disregard anything I might have said in the first paragraph...) and started excavating in a precise and controlled manner. Within minutes of removing the first few bits of soil, we hit literally hundreds of jasper taconite flakes and partially completed and broken tools lying within inches of the ground surface. As we expanded the excavation area, it became clear that during our initial testing we'd somehow managed to straddle large areas which were absolutely plastered in artifacts. Instead of a tiny camp or a single use chipping area, we were in the middle of a tool making workshop. Debris from the manufacture of countless tools was all around.

Almost immediately it was obvious that the budget would never allow us to complete that scale of work at the rate we were able to proceed.

Virtually every artifact we recovered during the excavations was made of that lovely jasper taconite. Most were flakes – the by-products which fly off during the refinement of a blank of rock down to something that can made into a knife, scraper or spear point. They are the equivalent of a carver's wood chips, except sometimes the flakes themselves would be selected for refinement and used as tools. A smaller number of artifacts were what archaeologists call bifaces. These are chunks of rock from which flakes have been systematically removed on both sides – it is part of the thinning and refinement process which ultimately leads to a workable tool. Most of the bifaces we recovered were broken or appeared to have been discarded after the 'knapper' had taken a couple of experimental whacks at it to see whether it was going to be easy to work further. These folks were close to an almost inexhaustible supply of jasper taconite, so they didn't waste their time with any pieces that were going to give them trouble.

Other than a handful of large granite cobbles that had been used as hammer stones, there were precisely two artifacts which stood out from the rest because they were not only of different material, but they were complete, finished objects.

The first of these was a rather nice drill bit made from very fine grained silicified siltstone. The other – and really a most spectacular find – was a small spear point made of an unusual dark orange silicified sandstone.

This artifact was a long way from home. The source of 'Hixton Silicified Sandstone' is in south-western Wisconsin, approximately 400 miles to the south-west of Thunder Bay. Furthermore, the spear point had clearly had a long hard life. From the shape of the blade, we could tell that it had started life as a much longer spear point, but either through breakage or resharpening, the blade had been worked until it was little more than a nub. From the shape of the base and the way the flakes had been carefully removed, we knew it was similar to Eden/Scottsbluff points – Late Palaeo Indian spear points found throughout much of the continental US and which are roughly 9250 and 8800 years old.

Whether it had been acquired by locals people through trade with others living to the south, or whether people from the Thunder Bay area migrated south each year to avoid the harsh winters, we can only speculate.

Now, here comes the sad part of the story. Like many people involved in archaeology, from time to time I would give presentations to school classes or talks to history groups. Usually I would take some artifacts with me to show around and to stimulate questions and conversation. A teacher at our local grade school invited me to come and talk to his class as they had just finished a section on Indigenous Peoples. A talk about archaeology was a natural fit.

I showed them a few slides then passed around some artifacts. At the end of the class we packed everything up, I went home and thought about it no further.

Some months later, one of my colleagues was visiting, so I showed him a few of the more interesting artifacts I have excavated over the years. I'm generally careful about keeping artifacts in their right bags and boxes, but when I went to find the Hixton spear point, it was nowhere to be found. I have searched for it many times since, but the only conclusion I can come to is that some little rotter palmed it during the school presentation.

We worked long, hard diligent days on that project, but eventually we ran out of resources and had to return home. I was faced with cleaning, cataloguing, analyzing and reporting on a collection of over 26,000 artifacts – many of which were tools or tool blanks in various stages of production. The remaining budget ensured that I would be paid far less than minimum wage, yet I had a legal and moral obligation to complete the work.

I learned a number of important lessons at this site: never make assumptions based on insufficient information; always do additional testing before preparing a budget; and, if you show artifacts to school kids, always, always, always double check that you have them all back at the end of the class.

The English River

Bill Bryson is a great travelling companion. Steve and I were rolling north in my bus[6], taking it in turns to drive while the other read out loud from Bill's new book 'A Walk in the Woods'. Bill's infectious humour was helping the long miles pass and it somehow seemed appropriate that we too were passing through endless woods.

We were heading north to do some survey work on the English River in advance of a proposed mine. It sounded straight-forward: do some basic survey in the vicinity of the mine site, find some archaeological sites in the area so these could be protected and managed from any secondary impacts. Development always results

---

6   *I'd replaced my truck with a 1 ton, dual wheel diesel 'shorty' ex-school bus.*

in increased activity – this way, the places to avoid could be factored in to the planning.

Having completed our work on the Mississagi River a couple of years before, we were convinced of the value of using a canoe to do the survey along the river. A boat may help you to get from one place to the next at speed, but it didn't give you the same perspective of the landscape as travelling by canoe. By using the same tools at the same speed as the areas original inhabitants, we believed we saw the landscape in the same way.

When we arrived at the mining exploration camp, the various geologists and planners already there were a bit surprised to see our mode of transportation, and over supper we answered the usual questions about what we were looking for and how we went about it. I think it's fair to say we encountered some mild scepticism.

The English is a big, wide, island filled river which extends from the Winnipeg River east into central north-western Ontario. It was a major fur trade route, connecting the prairies to Hudson's Bay by the Albany River. We were only going to be looking at a tiny section in the vicinity of the mine site, but even that involved quite a few miles of shoreline.

After spending the night in one of the canvas tents, we woke early and walked over to the 'mess' tent for some coffee and breakfast. Tom, one of the geologists was already there and offered us some Raisin Bran as he poured himself a bowl. Steve demurred, opting for some toast and peanut butter, but I thought that some breakfast cereal sounded perfect. Tom poured some for me too then started eating. After a couple of mouthfuls he stopped, taking his bowl outside where the light was better. I was just about to pour my milk when Tom said,

"Wait – don't eat that".

In the better light outside he'd been able to see why his cereal didn't taste quite right; it was absolutely peppered with mouse droppings. I didn't need much encouragement to throw mine away, opting to follow Steve's example and eat some toast, but Tom, who was clearly made of sterner stuff, opened a new box of Raisin Bran, poured himself another bowl, and carried on eating.

Over the next couple of days, Steve and I slowly and systematically searched the area, preferring to camp out on one of the islands rather than returning to the mining camp each night.

When we did finally return, the camp crew were shocked to see the artifacts representing about 8000 years of human occupation, that we had recovered from places they knew well and had visited often. Their concern about us using the canoe rapidly faded.

Later on, as part of the same project, we accompanied Mike, a planner, to the two local First Nations reserves affected by the project, to introduce our study and explain our work to councillors and Elders. We had picked up a representative of the Bimose Tribal Council in Kenora (I'll call him George) who was to going to accompany us to the Wabaseemoong (White Dog) First Nation. As it was a long ride in the bus, we had plenty of time to chat and relax – at least, as relaxed as we could be in a hard sprung bus bouncing over unpaved roads.

After many miles, George said,

"Just turn off down this little road to the right and wait. We have to meet someone."

We turned the corner down a little sandy track, pulled to the side and waited. After about ten minutes, a pickup truck arrived and a large native guy got out and headed towards us. Mike started to introduce us, but he was immediately interrupted.

"I know who you are, and I have been instructed by my council and Elders not to allow you entry on to our territory."

He explained that the community did not feel that the mining company had been consulting with them in an appropriate way, and until they were satisfied with the process, we, nor any of the mining project's staff or consultants were not allowed access to their territory.

Once he realized we weren't going to argue the point, the mood thawed considerably and we were able to have a pleasant chat. He knew our part to was to look for archaeological sites, something he was personally interested in, having spent some time at Trent University studying archaeology and anthropology, but his current job was to stop our arrival.

Wabaseemoong was one of two communities which had been disastrously affected by mercury and other neurotoxins dumped into the English-Wabigoon Rivers by a paper mill during the nineteen sixties. Many band members suffered a variety of neurological and sensory problems, broadly described as Minimata disease – named after a small fishing community in Japan where mercury poisoning had devastated the community.

Not surprisingly, the people at Wabaseemoong were suspicious of any industrial activity which might affect their community and were determined to ensure that their concerns were fully addressed through appropriate consultation. Steve and I promised not to conduct any more survey within Wabaseemoong territory until their issues with the company had been resolved.

The following day we had another meeting scheduled, this time with representatives of the adjacent Asubpeeschoseewagong First Nation (Grassy Narrows). These people had also been terribly affected by the toxins in the English-Wabigoon River. This time, however, we drove in to the community without being stopped and were soon led in to a meeting room.

After we were all comfortably seated around a large table and the introductions were completed, Mike was asked to explain the hazards and benefits of the mine. He started well, talking about jobs for community members and the potential social benefits in clear, concise language. At such meetings the person with the floor is allowed to complete their talking without interruption, while the Elders and councillors quietly listen, usually looking down, and not at the speaker. If you are used to plenty of eye contact while giving presentations, this can be a little unsettling, almost to the point where you think nobody is listening. Nothing could be further from the truth. When Mike finished, the youngest person in the room, a guy of perhaps 20 or 21, said, (and bare in mind that this was 1998, and the internet was still young)...

"Tell us about your company's toxic spill in Venezuela and why we should believe something similar couldn't happen here."

You hear about people's jaw dropping in surprise, but I'd never actually seen it happen before. To give Mike credit, he quickly recovered and managed to give a satisfactory explanation of the specific geological circumstances surrounding the Venezuela operation, which made it unlikely that a similar event could happen here, but he was completely blind-sided. It was an important lesson in not making any assumptions about the knowledge, or access to information of the people to whom you are speaking.

Later on in the same meeting, an Elder named Mary, who was one of those twinkly eyed Grandmotherly types you just wanted to hug, talked calmly about how the mine would be finished in 30 years or so, and the company would just move on, whereas her people would be there for ever, with just a hole in the ground to show for it. When your people been living somewhere for thousands of years, you take the long view.

The road in to the Reserve had a been a long, bumpy ride along a rutted gravel road. My poor bus had absorbed quite a shaking. On the way back we noticed that some of the screws holding the dashboard had backed right out of their holes, one of two of them even ending up on the floor.

Just after screwing most of them back in to place, we rounded a corner to find a mother bear and three cubs ambling along the side of the road. We stopped to watch, but mother gave us a look which said,

"Move along now, we don't want any trouble – and whatever you do, don't get out of that bus."

She didn't need to tell us twice. We left them in peace.

The Frog

We were just going through the motions really, digging the prescribed number of holes along the edge of the Little Cataraqui Creek valley, not really expecting to find anything, doing our due-diligence, when 'magic-boots' Phil found some pottery in his test pit.

The area we were working in was part of the large limestone plain which surrounds Kingston and extends west along the shores of Lake Ontario. It's generally flat land. Where the soils are thick enough, the land is cultivated. Where there is only a skim of soil above bedrock, it's left in scrubby forest. During the last glaciation, ice scoured a broad, wide valley, but the stream which now occupies it is a trifling little thing, far too small even to navigate by canoe. There were various terraces down near the creek. That's where we expected to find archaeological sites, not up there on the valley edge.

In other parts of southern Ontario, high valley edges overlooking a wide, swampy valley would have immediately been identified as having high archaeological potential for Late Woodland period, pre-Contact Iroquois villages. But in the

Kingston area there were no old reports of finds, not even rumours, and we had assumed, quite wrongly as it turned out, that our chances of finding anything so high above and so far from the creek, were few. Finds from the same period had been found in the region, but they were limited to small camp sites on the margins of the lakes and rivers.

Other positive test pits soon followed. Before long we had a large enough sample of artifacts that we were able to determine that the site dated to the 14th or 15th century. Iroquoian pottery has very distinctive designs which changed subtly through time and which provide a reliable, if rough and ready way to date the site.

As with other projects, this one proceeded through a number of stages, designed for the archaeologist to gain a good picture of the extent of the site before committing to preserving or excavating it. At first, we thought the occupation area was restricted to a relatively narrow band along the valley edge, but after machining off the plough-zone in the field to the rear, we were able to see and map a host of small post-holes which defined the locations of buildings. Sadly one side of the site had already been built upon, during a prior phase of the Arbor Ridge housing development, at a time when archaeological assessments had not been required. The other side had been destroyed by a small limestone quarry, thus our excavations were restricted to the bit remaining in the middle.

But first a bit of context. The people who lived on either side of Lake Ontario in the 14th and 15th centuries shared much in common. They lived in large, often palisaded villages, hamlets and fishing camps, often surrounded by many acres of cleared land where they grew corn and other crops. They built multi-family 'longhouses'. They made distinctive clay cooking and storage pots and smoking pipes, and they often lived in a state of tension with their neighbours. They spoke distinct, but mutually intelligible languages, and shared many cultural characteristics, including blood feuds and captive adoption.

Villages were occupied for a short period of time - on average between 10 and 30 years - before the soil they were using to grow crops lost its fertility, the distance from fire wood supplies and the condition of longhouse structures necessitated village movement.

Usually, if there's one village in the area, there are more[7].

As we excavated along the valley edge it was soon clear that we were dealing with a large midden – a village refuse dump. Excavations at other Late Woodland Iroquoian villages almost always encounter middens. They are usually positioned near the ends of longhouses where debris from broken pots, fish skins and skeletons, old bones, ash from fires and, well, any other nasty stuff, could be safely dumped. They are treasure for archaeologists.

The soils within the midden contained hundreds of pieces of pottery, bone tools, broken pipes and a host of organic materials including fish scales and vertebrae, pieces of turtle carapace, freshwater mussel shell as well as larger bones from dog, beaver, deer and bear. Fish, turtle and shellfish are most easily acquired during the summer, while bear and deer can be hunted at any time of year – was this a summer settlement?

We started to think about why the people had chosen that spot. Some Iroquoian villages were situated with an eye to defence, but we had found no traces of a defensive stockade or palisade wall, and the site backed on to open country. Being on the valley edge may have given some advantage over anyone attacking from below, but enemies could have easily approached from the rear. The site provided a clear, unimpeded view of bay where the creek flowed in to Lake Ontario. But while they would have been able to see any enemies passing along the lake shore, their cooking fires and perhaps even the longhouse at the valley edge, would also have been visible. I was left with the impression that security and obscurity were not high on their priority list.

The lower part of the creek flows in to an extensive marsh near the big lake. This area, which is a short walk away across well drained land, would have been very attractive to the inhabitants – full of fish, muskrats, turtles, beavers and wild fowl. Perhaps this was the attraction.

As excavation and recording of the post-holes proceeded, the clear outline of one longhouse and parts of two more began to emerge. The main longhouse was no small structure. It was at least twenty-five metres long and roughly seven metres wide – large

---

7   *Just recently, almost 20 years after we discovered the Arbor Ridge site, evidence of what may be a second Iroquoian village in the Kingston area was discovered.*

enough to house at least five families. Most longhouses that have been excavated have fire pits at regular intervals along the centre-line of the building. At our longhouse, this was not the case. The interior of the structure was remarkably free of pits and hearths, making us wonder whether it was mainly used for sleeping and the cooking was done outside. Certainly we found a number of fire pits which didn't seem to relate to the interior of any dwellings. Perhaps it was just too darn hot and sticky to cook inside.

Analysis of the artifacts occurred in two phases. At the end of the excavation I quickly compiled a summary report so that the developer could get clearance to proceed with the construction project. The main analysis had to wait a few years until there was a bit of a break in the work stream. I'm still not completely finished the final report, but soon........

The analysis is complete though. After sorting through all the pottery I was able to identify 148 separate pots, based on the distinctive ways in which the rim and neck areas were decorated. Archaeologists have come up with a variety of ways to describe these patterns of decoration, using names such as: Pound Necked, Salem Horizontal, Middleport Criss-Cross and others. These types have become entrenched in the archaeological literature and anyone studying Iroquoian pottery learns to recognize them. More recently 'attribute analysis' has become *de rigueur,* where a mass of individual characteristics (lip form, lip decoration, lip notching collar shape, collar decoration etc. etc.) are described and tabulated. The idea is that this approach is free from mi-identification. That's the idea anyway.

When I compared the pots from Arbor Ridge with pottery from a host of other archaeological sites in Ontario and adjacent parts of New York State, a number of things emerged. Firstly, the people at Arbor Ridge were making pottery which was very similar to that being made by Huron people along the Lake Ontario shore to the west, and virtually nothing like pottery made by people to the east. It was as if the Arbor Ridge site was a frontier settlement, on the very edges of the Huron world. Secondly, it had always been assumed that there was tension and fear between people living on either side of the river, yet our research suggested that on the contrary, there may have been quite close ties between the Arbor Ridge people and the St. Lawrence Iroquois living to the south – a notion supported by the evident lack of concern for defence.

In the past, the main story about the people who lived at the eastern end of Lake Ontario during the Late Pre-Contact period was one of danger, hostility, warfare, torture and capture.

The analysis of the pottery from Arbor Ridge and its neighbouring sites, suggests a different plot line. In this new story, two culturally related, but distinct peoples lived side by side in relative harmony, trading, sharing a broad territory, perhaps even living in each other's villages.

As the people even further to the south - the Five Nations Iroquois - consolidated their power and established a political union along the south shore of Lake Ontario, they began to feel vulnerable. A few villages from the eastern end of the region distanced themselves from the threat by moving their villages across the St. Lawrence River, or joined their relatives further down- stream. The majority however, chose to gradually move west to join with their Huron allies to the north of Lake Ontario and in the Trent River valley.

Although sherds of pottery were by far the most common objects found at Arbor Ridge, there were other artifacts including some decorated bone points and awls, part of a ground stone adze, a few chert flakes and tools, and some clay pipe parts. Only two stone arrowheads were found and while this may seem surprising, it wasn't unexpected. The Kingston area doesn't really have a good local source of raw material for chipping arrowheads; it either has to be acquired through trade or some other solution was sought. At Arbor Ridge, the people used the raw material they had plenty of – bone. A bone arrow point is just as effective as a stone one, and bone, from the various animals that ended up in the stew pot, was readily available.

Smoking pipes are common on sites of this period, and Arbor Ridge was no exception. These are hand made clay pipes, with carefully moulded bowls and a short stem or mouthpiece. They bowls are conical, vase-shaped, barrel-shaped or flaring like a trumpet. Some are plain, but many are decorated with the same kinds of incised patterns as the cooking pots.

One of the questions archaeologists are often asked is:

"What was your most exciting or interesting find?"

Forget about swords and Anglo-Saxon jewelry, Roman coins or

exotic arrowheads. Mine came from Arbor Ridge. It was broken and incomplete, but it speaks to me in a way no other artifact I've encountered ever could. You're probably going to think I'm crazy – but my favourite, most precious, most wonderful thing is a tree frog, crawling around the bowl of a clay pipe.

We only have part of it. The head and the front legs are missing, although we managed to identify a few toes amid the piles of pottery fragments, but from the small pieces we have, you can tell that the frog was lovingly moulded on to the surface of the pipe. It's face would have been peeping around the bowl at the smoker. It's whimsical and charming.

Little things like this really connect us to the past. Whoever made that pipe had observed tree-frogs carefully, then humorously made it part of his daily life. Archaeologists spend so much time talking about survival strategies, economies and techno-traditions of the people whose remains they study as if life was only about survival and practical choices. They forget about laughter, love, joy, happiness and fun. There's nothing practical about this frog. It speaks to me of warm, summer evenings, of contentment, of quietly smoking while looking out across the valley as the sun goes down, of children playing king-of-the-castle on the midden heap, of bullfrogs booming in the wetland and nighthawks calling overhead. It's pure joy.

CHAPTER 6

THE DAILY GRIND

Much of the work contract archaeologists do is, frankly, a bit boring. A client sends us plans or maps of the area they are going to obliterate, we come up with a price to conduct the work in accordance with the provincial standards and guidelines, then we get on with it. Because the places scheduled for modern development don't always coincide with the areas selected for settlement and occupation in the past, we sometimes find very little and sometimes nothing. Nevertheless, we have to perform the work in an appropriate manner, so that both the client and the various regulatory and review agencies can have confidence in the results.

Often this means spending days - weeks sometimes - working through tangled bush and thick forest, digging little holes, sifting dirt, and systematically covering the whole area, even when we know there's little chance of stumbling onto anything noteworthy or interesting. At times like this, it pays to be working with people with good conversational skills. It's hardly Indiana Jones stuff, although we do have to fight our way through prickly ash, poison ivy, and brave deadly, low hanging wasps nests.

Which reminds me of a story.

Bob's Lake is a huge, many-armed lake not far from where I now live. Our client had bought a large section of land with the plan to build some luxury houses overlooking the water. This is Canadian Shield country; visualize glacially smoothed rocky outcrops, areas of swamp and alder, steep slopes down to the lake shore, heavy forest, and a few patches of meadow. Because of the bedrock, the trees aren't actually all that large, but they stick their roots wherever they can find enough soil to grow, sometimes emerging out of the cracks and crevices.

We were a small crew that day - just Steve, Christopher[8] and me. Christopher is stocky, short and immensely strong. He's built like a weight lifter, but his muscle and bulk come from hard work and genetics, not from hours in the gym. Although he's pleasant, cheerful and endlessly kind and generous, you just know it would be a really bad idea to tangle with him. He's one of those rare guys that can defuse an awkward situation just by his presence and his calm manner. He has been called a human bulldozer, but ironically, he can also be extremely careful when excavating something delicate. Like Steve, he's been working with me for years.

As usual, my dog was along for the day. It was Jenny – a strange, lovely little beast, a bit like a cross between a German Shepherd and a Muppet.

Steve and I were working along the edge of the slope. Christopher and Jenny were close together at the water's edge. While Christopher probed at a little patch of soil between the rocks, Jenny decided to pull on a branch sticking up from a rotten log. Suddenly she yelped and raced off along the shore. Seconds later, Christopher let out an even louder yelp, dropped his shovel and screen and ran too. About every five yards he would yelp again and take a little jump as wasps streamed after him. He was stung about six times, each time punctuated by his high pitched yowl, before he was far enough from their nest that they gave up. To see such a robust guy shrieking like a little girl was desperately funny and we've tormented him by retelling the story many times, but there was a darker side.

Unfortunately, Christopher is allergic to wasp stings and we were a long way from help, so for the next couple of hours we kept a careful eye on him. Steve assured him that he would happily use

---

8   *We usually call him Chris, but I don't want you to confuse him with my wife (I don't want to be confused either….).*

his Swiss Army knife to do an emergency tracheotomy if the need arose, but I'm not sure his offer helped. After this little scare, Christopher always has an Epipen in his field kit, and while we've had more than our fair share of wasp encounters, so far, we haven't had to use it.

The Great Fire

Many basic survey projects end up being so similar that they all blend together after a while – especially if nothing of note was discovered and no memorable event - such as Christopher's 'fun with wasps', happened to fix it in our memories. One or two stand out though because they brought something unexpected to light.

We had been contracted to complete the archaeological assessment of a large section of land near Ottawa. Let me tell you, 700 acres of tightly-packed bush and swamp is a lot of land if you have to walk every inch of it and dig holes in most of it.

Before we started, as we always do, we did some basic background research into the property to determine whether there were any known archaeological sites in the area and to gather some information on its geology, topography, and historical settlement. Two maps were particularly useful. Both the 1863 'Walling map' of Carleton County and the map in the 1878 Historical Atlas of Carleton County showed three nineteenth century farmsteads on our patch of land, even though none of the later maps and plans showed any standing buildings.

From past experience, we were fairly certain we would be able to find these former dwellings. There are usually surface clues: old cellar pits, often filled with modern rubbish, and lilacs bushes and apple trees often betray old farmsteads, even when little else is visible. Still, we relegated these to the back of our minds and got on with the arduous business of breaking 700 acres down into manageable chunks which we could survey and test in a systematic manner.

The first job was a bit of exploration to familiarize ourselves with the property and eliminate any areas where the archaeological potential was so low that any investment of time would be futile. This part of Ontario is a peculiar world of flat, forested limestone plains, interspersed with areas of swamp. Since the swamps have been there since the demise of the last ice age, we could eliminate those – but not before we'd traversed their boundaries on foot and could map them with some degree of accuracy. We spent a long day sploshing around in knee deep water before we were content that we had a good handle on what was land, what was swamp, and which parts might be either depending on the season.

In places the soil cover over the bedrock was very thin and in some places was missing altogether. These 'alvar' areas were thinly covered with mosses and the occasional juniper bush and were difficult to test effectively. No one could conceivably have found them an attractive place to be.

Much of the rest of the property was maple and mixed spruce-maple forest, with reasonably deep soils, or forested land that graded gradually towards the swamps and would be waterlogged during high-water conditions. Our physiographic and soils maps also showed a narrow band of sand running diagonally across the property. This marked the shoreline of the Champlain Sea - a vast brackish expansion of the St. Lawrence River estuary - that extended inland, filling up most of what is now the Ottawa River valley, about 11,000 years ago. Since people were living in Ontario by that time, it's reasonable to assume that these ancient shorelines could have been occupied, although there is little conclusive evidence yet to prove they did. Nevertheless, it was something we had to test thoroughly.

As the days and weeks wore on, we gradually tested all the testable areas, and dutifully located and recorded all three historic farmsteads. Actually, we found four.

During our background research we had investigated the census records for each property, adding information to the notations available from the maps. In the process, we discovered that although only the three dwellings were indicated on the maps, the census records suggested that there might be a fourth, occupied by a tenant farmer, so it was no great surprise when we found the remains of his house.

In this part of Ontario, Irish and Scottish settlers first moved into the area in the 1820s and. most nineteenth century farmsteads are regarded as having some archaeological significance.

Life in these farmsteads would have been immensely tough. Hacking a farm out of virgin forest involved vast amounts of physical labour and privation until enough land was cleared to grow a few crops and graze a few cattle. Contemporary illustrations often show a tiny log cabin or shanty, surrounded by tree stumps with a few wispy crops growing in between. In the early years, roads were little more than muddy cart tracks between the surveyed concessions.

Many of the settlers in Carleton County arrived as part of immigration programs, and were assigned land and provided with tools and support for the first few months to get them started. Many more were not, but came anyway, fleeing conditions in Ireland and Scotland, looking for a better life. What they found was unremitting labour, clouds of insects, vicious, long winters, and often as not, poor-quality soils. At least they didn't have hostile natives to content with too. The Algonquins, on whose territory they were settling, were few in number, and generally peaceful with their new neighbours.

Astonishingly, despite being unused to the environment, most managed to eventually make a living. One of the sites we tested had been occupied by John Wright and his family. Wright was in the area by the 1830s and by the early 1840s had settled on the property we were assessing. Agricultural census returns for 1861 show that by that time he had managed to clear 20 acres for crops, had 30 acres of pasture land and was living in a log house with his wife Ellen and family.

One of the most delightful characteristics of the Ottawa valley is that many log buildings have survived from the days of the early settlers. In areas where the soil was good and farming was profitable, it's not unusual to see a rather grand brick or stone farmhouse surrounded by log barns and smaller outbuildings. It's sometimes possible to recognize the original log house – perhaps now in use as a tractor shed – or the first shanty, now occupied by pigs or chickens.

In the more marginal areas, some of the log houses are still occupied, or stand neglected in the corner of a field. It's astonishing how small they are, often little more than 12' by 16', yet many of them housed large families for many years.

At first, we didn't even find a cellar pit or foundation where the Wright's house had stood, although the artifacts in our test pits gave us some idea of where the house had been and a picture of it's occupants. These were not rich people. The pots, bowls and plates they used were plain and cheap; there were no fancy dinner parties occurring at the Wright's house. Virtually everything we found was for practical use: nails, various bits of metal hardware, hinges and staples. One of the adults was a smoker; there were plenty of 'churchwarden style' white clay pipe pieces. It seems to have been their only luxury.

As our testing proceeded, we encountered large areas of dark staining and fragments of burned wood surrounding a hard platform of rocks and the remains of the stone footings which had supported the log house sills. The house had stood on a low knoll, overlooking a large swamp. It would have been safe from flooding, but not from the hoards of mosquitoes breeding in the slow-moving water.

When we analyzed the artifacts, it became clear that people had ceased to live there during the last third of the 19th century. We looked at the documentary records again, this time noticing that the Wrights had continued to hold a mortgage on the land until 1880, but whether they were actually living there that late didn't seem likely. Certainly nothing in the artifact assemblage suggested that they had stayed there after 1870.

One of the poorly recorded yet historically significant events ever to affect the Ottawa valley, was the 'Great Fire of 1870'. In order to set the scene for this, you have to imagine a tinder dry landscape of forest, small clearings, and farms. All the buildings are log with cedar shingle roofs, and vast amounts of dry brush from clearing and felling are lining the farm fields. Many of the buildings and all the fence lines, are made entirely from cedar – a highly resinous, combustible wood. Now add in hot August temperatures, a persistent drought, strong winds, and the widespread use of fire for heat, light, cooking, and for clearing fields, and you have the perfect recipe for disaster.

A crew working on clearing the new Central Canada Rail line between Almonte and Pakenham had set some small fires along the route to get rid of the brush, but strong winds almost immediately whipped them out of control. Within minutes, the fire was racing with the wind. As some contemporary accounts record, the fire front was advancing 'at the speed of a trotting horse'. Flaming debris was sucked up with the wind, and thrown around, starting new fires in all directions.

Despite mighty efforts to curtail it, the fire was soon completely out of control. Over the following days, the area affected grew unimaginably large, burning over thousands of square kilometres. Unable to flee the fire, people sought refuge down their wells, in rivers and lakes, or even buried themselves in their green-crop fields. Sometimes they were lucky. Despite the sparsely populated landscape, over 3,000 farms were destroyed, thirteen people were killed and thousands of people became instant refugees.

The village of Stittsville, about 3 kilometres east and the closest settlement to the Wright's house was almost completely destroyed. Ottawa was only saved because someone had the brilliant idea to release some of the water from the dam at Dow's Lake. A channel was cut so the water could flow down to Nepean Bay, creating a fire break. To the west of Stittsville, the huge tamarack swamps, parts of which lay within our study area, burned with particular violence.

Given their proximity to Stittsville and the swampy lands, it is inconceivable that any of the small farmsteads on our property escaped unscathed. Indeed, the evidence of burning we found at each location strongly suggests they didn't.

Whether the Wrights returned to their property to survey the damage, once the fires had burned themselves out, is unclear. Their house was gone, their outbuildings were gone, their tools, livestock, seeds, and everything else of value, were consumed. We have no record of how they, or their neighbours managed to survive after the fire, but the archaeological evidence indicates that only one of the four farmsteads was re-occupied after 1870. The lands which had been cleared and farmed after such a massive expenditure of time and physical effort, were abandoned and forgotten.

Small is beautiful

When I started in archaeology, if there was a conflict between development and archaeological resources, salvage excavation was the default response. Archaeologists considered themselves lucky if they were granted a little time to do some hurried salvage before the sites were destroyed forever. It was at the whim of the developer.

In the last few decades we have come a long way. Archaeological surveys in advance of development, mandated and regulated by government, and paid for by the developers, are a normal part of the development process. Most of the larger development companies are used to it. They recognize that if they want to change the world in order to make a profit, they have a responsibility to deal with whatever was there first in an appropriate way. Usually the cost of archaeology is a tiny fraction of their overall budget and rarely makes a dent in the bottom line. From time to time you hear a bit of whining - usually from small scale developers or 'first timers' - but most accept this as a normal, and quite reasonable requirement, no different from conforming to zoning by-laws or maintaining setbacks from creeks and rivers.

Not long ago, if a site was identified in advance of development, it almost always got dug. These days, there is a far greater emphasis on preservation, indeed, in Ontario, our provincial 'Standards and Guidelines' emphasize that avoidance and protection is always the preferred approach. This can be achieved by redesigning the project to avoid sensitive areas, by excluding the site from the development area altogether, or by incorporating the archaeological site into open spaces, parks or woodland areas which will remain free from future development.

But............ it's not always practical.

During testing of a lakeshore property in eastern Ontario, we found a very small group of artifacts on the surface of a ploughed and weathered field overlooking the lake. Actually, at first we found precisely two artifacts: a small chert flake and a heavily abraded piece of native pottery. It wasn't much to go on, but it was enough to trigger a more intensive surface survey in that area.

There was a time, not so long ago, when archaeologists believed that their research interests trumped any concerns that First

Nations people may have had about the remains left by their ancestors. Fortunately, those days are long gone. We have an ethical and regulatory duty to consult with the closest First Nations groups whenever detailed testing on archaeological sites containing aboriginal artifacts are planned.

I had been in contact with with the Algonquins of Ontario from the outset of the project, to inform them that the initial survey was about to occur. This information was circulated to Chief Doreen Davis of the Shabot Obaadjiwan First Nation, the closest First Nations group, who phoned me to express her interest and desire to be kept up-to-date on our progress and results. As soon as we found any aboriginal artifacts, I contacted her to describe the finds and outline the next stages.

The more intensive survey - literally searching the ground surface on our hands and knees - turned up another 11 artifacts within an area about the same size as an average backyard swimming pool. Of the 11 artifacts, 9 were little chips of chert - the by-product from making or sharpening stone tools. The other two were the tip of an arrowhead and the base of second. It still wasn't much to go on, but the provincial regulations stipulate that if even a single piece of aboriginal ceramics is found, Stage 3 (detailed testing) is required.

The purpose of Stage 3 testing is to gain a larger sample of artifacts and to see what, if anything, is preserved within and below the plough soil. The hope is that by digging a series of 1 metre square test units on a five metre grid, you will be able to define the extent of the site, and gain a better understanding of its age and heritage value. Once the extent of the site has been determined, this information can be used to work with the developer to come up with a plan to protect the site, or if that's not possible, to excavate it.

Our Stage 3 work soon showed that the site was very small. The artifacts we recovered were limited to an elliptical area of less than 20 metres by 25 metres. Whatever had been taking place there was clearly on a small scale.

The developer was intending to divide the property into a small number of building lots, each with a view of the lake. Our little site was precisely where they were planning to put one of houses. It was the prime location on the most expensive lot. Not surprisingly, preservation didn't seem like a viable option. To abandon that area would have rendered the prime lot unsaleable and jeopardized the viability of the whole plan. Since the area involved was so small, excavation was the only real option.

Excavation of the site consisted of two phases. The first phase was hand excavation of the main site area as determined during the Stage 3 testing. Following that, we used a flat-bladed digger to peel off the plough soil so that we could look for sub-surface features (pits, soils stains, preserved living floors etc.) which might have escaped damage by the plough. These were then carefully mapped and excavated.

When I describe the results you may not be wowed. In total we located and excavated three sub-surface features: one linear hearth or fire pit, and two smaller irregular shaped shallow pits. The total number of artifacts from the excavation, the Stage 3 testing, and the original surface survey was 430, most of which were tiny broken pieces of pottery with no decoration and limited research value.

So why am I making you waste your valuable time reading about this? Well, as I said in the book title, "Archaeology Ain't All Gold Masks and Crystal Skulls". Sometimes we have to look for meaning and value in what we have, not what we'd like.

When we looked closely at the pottery we were able to distinguish 9 separate vessels based on the rim sherds, almost all of which either came from within the linear hearth or were in the topsoil above or close by. Based on the rim shapes and design elements, they all dated to between A.D. 700 and A.D. 850[9] and are attributed to the Sandbanks Tradition - a transitional phase between the late Middle Woodland Period and the early Late Woodland Pickering phase.

If this all sounds like gibberish, don't worry. It just means that they date to the period in eastern Ontario archaeology when the mobile lifestyle of hunting, fishing and gathering was gradually being replaced by a more static, village and horticulture based economy.

But back to our site. Despite careful searching we didn't find any post-holes or stake-holes. These are small circular stains in the

---

9   *By seriation – a way of relative dating putting artifacts into chronological order.*

ground which show where support poles had once been dug into the earth. On some sites, it's common to find curved lines of post-holes, showing where wigwams or lodges had once stood. These were circular or oval dwellings made of bent saplings and covered with bark or skins. These almost always encircle a hearth or fire-pit, that would have been used for cooking and warmth. If they had existed at our site (as I'm sure they once did) all traces of them were probably removed during decades of ploughing.

That we had nine different vessels either suggests that whoever was cooking over that fire pit was extremely clumsy, or, as I prefer to believe, that the fire pit (and the assumed wigwam) was used over a number of seasons. We looked closely at the location.

The site is located on a terrace, well back from the lake shore and separated from the lake by a high bluff. This suggests that direct and easy access to the water was not a high priority. The whole area would probably have been heavily wooded, providing some protection from on-shore winds. It is hard to imagine that the location was chosen for defensive purposes or to provide some protection from observation. The location backs onto terrain with no natural defensive advantage and does not sit sufficiently far back from the lake shore to have been overlooked by someone determined to notice signs of human activity. It seems more likely that this location was chosen for defence against the climate: the trees along the lakeshore and the bluff would have provided a barrier to the wind, and the elevation above lake level may have provided some respite from the cold along the lakeshore. This line of reasoning suggest a cold-season occupation - perhaps where a single family wintered over a number of years. This might also partly explain the relative absence of sub-surface features and the number of broken pots.

One can imagine a small family group, returning year after year to the same location, perhaps leaving the (presumed) pole structure of their winter quarters intact and ready for re-use when required.

Such tiny, single or sporadic use archaeological sites may not be glamourous, but they are a very real part of the archaeological landscape, and in their own way, every bit as important as much larger sites. They give us a very small, hazy window through which to glimpse a few fragments of people's lives, all those hundreds of years ago.

CHAPTER 7

OF BONES AND BURIALS

One of the things we always include in our background studies for any development project is a search for burial and cemetery records. Although the Euro-Canadian settlement of Ontario is relatively recent, in the early years, people weren't always able to have their dead buried in formal cemeteries. There are many isolated burials and small family cemeteries dotted across the landscape. Some are marked and tended; most are abandoned and forgotten.

Over the years we have dealt with many historic burials. I regard this work as some of the most important we do.

Thomas and Jane's Last Home

We were working in the Ottawa area, testing in advance of a large development, when Chris found reference to a family plot on the property we were looking at. In his 1866 will, Thomas Wiggins specified that he wanted to be buried in his front garden. Furthermore, he wanted his wife, who had died three years earlier and who was buried in the Goulbourn graveyard a few miles away, to be dug up and buried along-side him. Thomas bequeathed 50 pounds to the Bishop of the diocese of Ontario to consecrate the burial ground and for the care and upkeep of his cemetery plot. The arrangement was never completed and the ground was never consecrated.

The family kept the burial area fenced and in good order until the property changed hands in the 1940's. There is a photograph showing grave stones and a white picket fence from just before the property was sold.

Clearly, the new owner was not interested in having a cemetery in his front garden. Some time shortly after the change in ownership, the fence and stones disappeared, and the burial area was forgotten.

Knowing where the burials should be made the job of locating them rather simple. As soon as we got out of the truck, we looked over to where my dog Jenny was sniffing at a groundhog burrow. The burrowing rodent had exposed the side of a large, dressed rock – it turned out to be one of the tomb stones.

We quickly laid out an excavation area, cleared the topsoil, and exposed part of the grave. The new owner had just pushed the stone over, covered it with a bit of soil and let the grass grow.

The natural subsoil in the area was a nice, stiff, yellow-orange sand. Anything that had ever been dug into it showed up with great clarity. By expanding our excavation area by machine, we were able to find the post holes where the picket fence had been, but where we were expecting to see two or more clear rectangular grave shafts filled with a mix of subsoil and topsoil, we found just one massive rectangular pit beneath the fallen stones.

Since we were about to dig into a human grave, we thought it prudent to contact the police to let them know what was taking place. Messing around with human remains is not something that can be undertaken lightly, and is regulated by various pieces of legislation.

However, unless we had actually encountered human remains, the police weren't interested. OK then.

'Doug, can you dig a test trench until you hit something?'

It took less than an hour before Doug encountered some fragments of coffin wood and vertebrae. We called the police back and showed them the bones.

"What are we supposed to do now?" the investigating officer said. I explained that we needed to contact the Cemeteries Registrar and that he would instruct us to conduct a formal investigation in order to provide him with full details about the number of bodies, the circumstances of their burial and their ages. He would then use that information to either register the area formally as a cemetery or require removal and reburial elsewhere.

A little while later, with our instructions from the registrar, we were back on site to do the full examination.

This time, we stripped off and cleaned up a broad area, then started to systematically investigate the large main feature, after determining there were no other burials in the area. After removing a metre and half of the feature fill, we encountered wooden planks set cross-wise (see cover photo). It was starting to get a bit confusing. After we recorded the planks, we removed them, and there below were two coffins, and the remains of Thomas and Jane Wiggins.

Our interpretation was that when Thomas died, he was placed in a standard coffin-shaped coffin, wearing a jacket with bone buttons. Jane's rectangular coffin, was dug up from the Goulbourn cemetery, bounced over to the new burial site in the back of waggon. Both coffins were then placed in one massive wooden box, which was then buried. They were together again as Thomas had desired.

Even before Sarah, our osteologist, started to examine the skeletons in detail, it was obvious that Thomas's last years must have been full of suffering. All his teeth were missing, and the holes where the teeth should have been had either grown over or had been enlarged where abscesses had eaten away at his jaw. His right arm would have been virtually useless from arthritis, and his back constantly ached. The bones in his lower back were degenerating.

Jane's body had been given a good shaking as it was carted over from Goulbourn. After three years of being in the ground, it would have been a bit sloppy and can't have smelled too good. The large box containing both coffins was probably designed to overcome this somewhat distressing reality.

Perhaps the pain Thomas suffered turned him in to a mean-spirited little man. As we continued to do historical research for other projects in the area, Thomas's name kept appearing in the records. He would buy up property deeds which hadn't been properly registered, turf the legitimate owners off their land simply because of their clerical oversight, and sell the land at a profit.

Thomas and Jane's grave was in the way of a massive new supermarket. Once we had completed our report, the Cemeteries Registrar decided that it made more sense to remove them and rebury them in the local Anglican church yard. It may have taken almost 150 years, but Thomas and Jane were finally buried in consecrated ground.

The Fate of Jacob Vosper

April can be a delightful month, with warm, sunny days and fresh new life bursting out everywhere. It can also be the cold, damp miserable tail-end of winter. This is how it was in 2003 when I got a call from Sue, one of my local colleagues, to help salvage and investigate some burials that had just been disturbed during renovations at the back of a church hall. The operator had been digging a basement hole for the extension to the hall with a large excavator when his dump truck driver noticed bones and large pieces of wood in the back of his truck.

The first order of business was to collect the surface bones and start screening the loose soil for other body parts. This sounds straightforward, but the heavy clay stuck to the bones, the coffin fragments, our boots, our clothes, and our skin. This might not have been so bad, except it stank. In the lowest part of the site, the burials had been dug into thick, waterlogged clay, which had slowed the natural process of decay. It smelled of death.

Once again, the main questions to be answered were: who were these people, how many burials were there, and were any still intact. These answers would help the Cemeteries Registrar decide their ultimate fate, thus the initial work was limited to establishing the locations and number of burials. Then, on instruction from the registrar, our job became one of removal for reburial.

While our historian searched the archives, looking for any information that might cast light on the cemetery, we got on with the messy business of dealing with the bodies.

Sue called in an osteologist from Queen's University who sat down with the buckets of bones we had collected from the machine-dug soil piles and started sorting them. It was fascinating to watch as she matched clavicles and femurs, grouping the bones into individuals based on their size, condition and morphology.

At the same time, we started to clear off the main area, and almost immediately, the distinctive shadow of a number of graves which had not been disturbed by the machine, became visible. This part of the site was easy to deal with using normal processes of recording and excavation. Some of the remains were moderately well-preserved within the rotted coffins; in others the remains were less robust, having succumbed to the effects of many years in the ground.

While we tried to get a handle on the mess left by the machines, we also had a swimming-pool sized disaster to deal with. In the days between the machine stopping digging and us starting the archaeological investigation, the hole for the basement had filled with a mix of rain and snow run-off, covering some of the areas we had to investigate with feet of foul and nasty water.

To drain the water, we hired a large sludge pump, ran a long line of hose out to the road and started it up. I have no idea how many hundreds and thousands of gallons of foul water we pumped in to the city storm drain but it was a lot. The pump kept chugging away, hour after hour, gradually lowering the water level until the area we needed to look at was just a gloopy mess of sticky, foul smelling mud. We tracked that mud everywhere we walked. Our muddy prints traced our regular break route from the site, along the sidewalk, to the nearest coffee shop.

While we were working on some of the higher burials, we watched as a large dog nearly pulled its owner off her feet in his eagerness to sniff a clump of that delicious, putrid goo. Doug was staying at my place while we worked at the site. Each night I hosed him down, while he stood, fully dressed, in the back yard. It took me ages to rid my work truck of the smell - the faint, but distinctive odour of corpse impregnated clay would resurface whenever it rained.

Many of the burials in the lower part of the site had been disturbed by the machine. Some had been almost completely removed, some had been cut in half. But one grave was completely intact.

Our historian Earl, had discovered that the land had been bought by the 'Union Church' (First Congregational Church and the Methodists) in 1827, for use as a burial ground. Records indicate that the last burials took place in 1875, after which it lay dormant. Three years later, the congregation decided to build a new brick church on the west corner of the burial ground. A few bodies were moved. Building on decommissioned grave yards was common practice at the time.

Over the years, additions and changes to the church probably displaced a few more bodies, but in the nineteenth century, nobody worried much about such things. As recently as the 1960s, bodies had been removed and reburied before a new wing of the church was added, but over the following 40 years, the existence of the cemetery appears to have been overlooked or forgotten.

It was hard for us to overlook though. The bodies made their presence felt through the odour of the clay and the uncomfortable tickling irritations in the back of our throats.

Other-Nick, Mike and Doug took on the delicate task of excavating the intact grave and cleaning around the undisturbed coffin, first packing their noses with Vics Vapour Rub against the appalling smell. They exposed the lid, then carefully excavated the thick clay around its edges. As they lowered the soil level adjacent to the coffin, putrid black, greasy water that had been sealed within streamed out and flowed around their boots.

Perhaps a little word of explanation is in order. Because the coffin was buried in heavy, wet clay, soon after the burial, whatever water could percolate down into the grave, found its way into the coffin. Gradually, as the soils within the grave shaft compacted, the coffin became surrounded and sealed by the thick clay. The natural process of decay began, but the cold water and lack of oxygen slowed it to a standstill.

Jacob was still in the box. Not just his bones, but great globs of greasy, grey, foul smelling goo. After removing the lid, Other-Nick reached down and gently touched the bulge at the head with his gloved hand (how I hope I remember he was wearing gloves!), and Jacob's whole scalp slithered off the back of his skull.

Since it was not going to be possible to extricate the coffin and its contents intact, Other-Nick carefully, and respectfully cleaned-off and gathered up all the bones, placing them in a special box for reburial.

The metal plate on the coffin identified Jacob. He was 53 years old when he died in 1849.

Once all the disturbed and intact burials had been recorded and the bones examined for age, gender and any unusual pathologies, they were boxed for reburial. I don't think any of us was unhappy when that project was over.

Bayview Cemetery

Not all of our dealings with human remains have been as grim. When we took on the job of doing the archaeological survey for a large property west of Kingston, the developers were already aware that there might be a small cemetery. Before the sale, the previous owner had mentioned it, and they had dutifully marked the area he had shown them on the development plans for protection.

As we started to examine the property in detail though, it was soon obvious that the area marked was in the wrong place. The soils in that area were only about a foot thick, sitting right on top of bedrock. It would have been virtually impossible to bury someone there. We set about looking for the real location.

It didn't take too long. While most of the land was farm fields, there was one small wooded area where the ground sloped towards the shores of Lake Ontario. As we worked through the tangled undergrowth, we started to notice some small, rounded pieces of natural limestone poking through. This in itself isn't unusual. Frost and tree roots can easily move rocks around, even bringing them to the surface in odd ways. These rocks were all aligned roughly north-south. We guessed that they were head stones, marking the locations of graves oriented east-west in the Christian pattern.

Chris had been doing the usual background research and had found out that although there was no cemetery registered with Cemeteries branch, some documents referred to a 'Bayview Cemetery" nearby. As she delved deeper, through often confusing and contradictory information, she determined that there were probably at least 6 people buried in the area, all members of the Rose family. The burials (if they existed at all) would date to the period between 1788 and 1832.

The developers were hoping to pass jurisdiction for the cemetery to the local municipality for permanent care. But obviously, they would not wish to transfer the burial site to the Township without some firm evidence that the area did indeed contain burials, nor would the municipality be prepared to take responsibility for its management when there was still doubt as to whether the area was indeed a burial site. Someone needed to demonstrate that there were graves in the ground – not just a bunch of odd rocks. That someone was us.

Our first task was to remove all surface vegetation from around the rocks and between the trees so that we could get a proper look at those mysterious rocks poking through the ground. Once we had a clear picture of the (presumed) orientation of the graves, we hand-excavated a series of metre wide trenches, laid out to intercept where we assumed the grave shafts would lie.

The topsoil in this forested area was quite thin and had never been ploughed. By skimming off the topsoil, we could expose the lighter coloured subsoil. If any graves were present, the grave shafts would show up as regular patches of slightly darker soil. And they did.

By this time, we were absolutely sure that we were working in the right place. The grave shafts were not only visible because of the soil colour; the tree roots had also sought out the softer, richer environment.

As a student, I had many summer jobs, but one of the best was working as a grave digger in the Robin Hood Municipal Cemetery in Solihull. On rare occasions, we would dig new, fresh graves in a previously unused part of the cemetery. Usually though, we would have to dig into existing graves.

Let me explain. Land is in short supply in England, but people are not, so if a family bought a burial plot, it would usually be a vertical space, designed to contain up to four coffins. When the first grave was dug, it would be far deeper than the 6 feet you always hear about, and the first coffin would be placed at the bottom, then the grave filled to the surface with soil. When the next family member died (sometimes soon after, sometimes many years later), we would re-excavated the grave until we encountered the previous coffin, leave a couple of inches of soil on top, then place the next coffin in the hole. And so on. We kept a special iron rod handy to push down into the ground to feel for the coffin lid when we thought we were getting close. Sometimes we misjudged, or the coffin lid collapsed, or.......... Being able to climb out of the hole really quickly, before you threw up, was a necessary skill.

Roots from the adjacent trees and bushes favoured the loose, rich, grave shaft soil, sometimes penetrating all the way down to the coffin, where they formed an almost impregnable matte.

If you've read about Mr. Wiggins above, you'll know that without the 'smoking gun' of human bone, none of the regulatory process to protect the cemetery could come in to play. It wasn't enough that we could show the locations of the graves and map the cemetery. We need to find some bones.

"Doug, can you just dig in to the head area of Grave G2 and expose some of the bones?"

Doug spent as much time chopping at tree roots as actually digging, but after a couple of hours he encountered fragments of coffin wood and iron nails about 4 feet below the ground surface. Long, thin lines of decayed wood showed where the vertical sides of the coffin had been (the lid having collapsed and rotted away) surrounding part of a skull. After 200 years of being in the ground, the pressure of the soil on the skull had caused it to collapse like an egg-shell. Doug cleaned and exposed it while I called the Ontario Provincial Police.

When the dispatcher answered the phone, the first thing I said was "This is nothing to get excited about", then I explained in some detail about the project.

Within minutes we could hear sirens in all directions as cruisers and unmarked police cars arrived, lights flashing, then a large forensic unit van turned up. The only things missing were the SWAT team and the dogs.

It didn't take the chief investigating officer long to realize this wasn't a crime scene. I showed him around the site explaining why we were here, how we worked, and why we'd called the dispatcher.

"The only thing that came over the radio was 'Human bones have been found in Amherstview'" he said.

Daft, mutton-headed dispatcher!

The police officers were actually quite relieved. They were on high alert as some much more recent and more suspicious human remains had been found in the area a few days earlier. They quite reasonably jumped to the conclusion that they had a killer on their hands.

"So what do I do now?" he asked.

I handed him a folder containing copies of our historical research and my communications with the Cemeteries Registrar.

"You need to call the coroner, to confirm that the remains are human and old, then it becomes a cemeteries issue," I said.

Eventually the coroner arrived. At first she had a hard time recognizing the broken piece of skull, which was still embedded in the ground, as human. As archaeologists, we get so used to mentally reconstructing situations, based on tiny fragments, that we forget that other people don't necessarily share our experience. Once I'd pointed out the headstones, shown her the discolourations indicating the grave shafts, and the wooden fragments and iron nails of the coffin, she was able to recognize the skull in it's broader context.

Once the existence of the burials had been established there was no further need to disturb the remains. The rest of the work focused on expanding our excavations until we knew the boundaries of the cemetery, and had a firm idea of the number of people buried there. By the end of the excavations we had documented 13 burials. Eventually I was able to submit our report to the Cemeteries Registrar who completed the process. The area is now fully fenced, protected and registered as a formal cemetery.

POSTSCRIPT

Archaeology has changed a lot in the last few years, at least in the little corner of the world in which I work. The days of being let loose on the world with a brand new truck, a canoe and a government credit card are long gone. In common with so many parts of modern society, we now operate in a world of regulation and conformity, where all archaeological reports end up looking basically the same, and where field practices are tightly controlled and managed.

Perhaps the more stringent requirements are leading to more consistent and better practices, but at the same time they are fossilizing archaeological technique, and limiting individual creativity. Governments now typically manage archaeologists, having long ago absolved themselves of any responsibility for managing archaeological sites. Nevertheless, we soldier on.

Working through old notes and photographs has dredged up many memories but has also re-energized my interest, and reminded me of things I have yet to do.

As you can probably tell from the little stories above, archaeological fieldwork can be physically demanding. It requires a certain level of fitness, yet at the same time it bestows it. Struggling through thick bush, shovel and screen in hand, stepping over fallen (often wasp filled) logs, digging and sifting is excellent all around exercise. It keeps the body strong and the mind alert.

People usually write this kind of personal retrospective when they are getting towards the end of their career. I don't feel that way at all. As far as I am concerned, I might be edging close to the mid-point. There are plenty of fields to walk and forests to struggle through yet.

I doubt whether there are any gold masks or crystal skulls in my archaeological future, and if you've been paying attention, you probably realize by now that it's not all about that anyway. Forget the pith hat and whip (you'll look like a dork anyway), you'll be better off with a bug net and a multi-tool.

No doubt there are archaeologists out there making the big discoveries and polishing up their National Geographic smile, while the rest of us – I dare say, most of us – are just plugging away with the grunt work. And that's just fine by me.

GLOSSARY OF TERMS

Adze: A ground stone tool, usually made of a hard rock, designed to be mounted in a wooden handle with the blade horizontal. These tools are thought to have been used mainly for woodworking – particularly for shaping dug-out canoes.

A.D. Abbreviation of the latin Anno Domini – of the Christian Era, or years passed since the birth of Christ.

Archaic: A term to designate cultural developments in North America between 7000 B.C. and 1,000 B.C.

Archaeology: The study of past cultures, usually through the materials they left behind.

Archaeological Excavation: The process and techniques used to examine and record locations of former human settlement and activity.

Archaeological Fieldwork: Any activity which involves the search for, examination and removal of archaeological materials.

Artifact: A product of human activity. Artifacts may range from manufactured materials such as stone tools and ceramics to bone and other refuse from food production.

Association: Artifacts found together in the same context are 'in association'.

Awl: A long narrow tool with a point at one end. These tools were often made of bone (more rarely of copper) and were used to punch holes in hides and other materials.

B.C.: Before Christ.

B.P.: Before present (where present is 1951 – the date from which radio-carbon assays are calibrated)

Biface: A stone tool which has been flaked on both sides.

Chert: A stone high in silica commonly used in the production of stone tools. Chert is either found as deposits in Palaeozoic rock formations or as nodules in glacial till.

Cord-wrapped stick: A term used to describe a type of decoration on pre-contact pottery. A thin stick, wrapped with braided cord is pressed sideways into the soft clay before firing to produce designs.

Debitage: Debris (flakes and chips) from the manufacture of flaked stone tools.

Feature: A term used to describe any modification to the ground (such as a storage pit, hearth or post-hole) which is visible as a change in soil colour, can be felt as a change in texture, or can be defined as a discrete concentration of artifacts.

Fire-cracked rock: Rocks which show clear alteration through heat (usually indicating old hearths or fire pits).

Flakes: Thin fragments of chert, chalcedony, rhyolite, quartzite, quartz, flint or other cryptocrystaline material which have been detached during the manufacture of flaked stone tools.

Gouge: A ground stone tool with a bevelled or channelled bit.

Gunflint: Small, deliberately shaped pieces of flint or chert which were held in the mechanism of flintlock rifles to produce a spark.

Grave Goods: Artifacts deliberately deposited with burials.

Lanceolate: Shaped like a lance point.

Late Woodland: A term used by archaeologists in North America to describe the final phase of the Woodland period – usually between A.D. 700 and A.D. 1650 (dates vary depending on geographical location – I've used Ontario dates). This period is usually associated with the rise in cultivation of crops and the emergence of villages.

Middle Woodland: A term used by archaeologists in North America to describe the middle phase of the Woodland period – usually between 500 B.C. and A.D. 700.

Multicomponent: A site that has been occupied by successive temporally or culturally unrelated groups.

Onondaga Chert: A blue-grey or whitish-grey chert found in outcrops in the Niagara Peninsula of Ontario and northern New York State.

Palaeo-Indian: This is the earliest phaseof human occupation in North America. In Ontario, it dates from approximately 10,000 B.C. to 7,000 B.C.

Pipe: A tool for smoking, usually consisting of a mouthpiece, stem and bowl and made of clay or stone. Pipes are often decorated.

Plano: A tradition of the Palaeo-Indian period extending from approximately 8,500 B.C. - 7,000 B.C.

Preform: An early stage in chipped stone tool production.

Prehistoric: Before written history. This term is no longer in widespread use in North America as it is perceived as derogatory to First Nations people. In the UK, it refers to the pre-Roman period.

Projectile Point: Arrows, spear or dart tips. Points are made from a variety of materials including stone and bone.

Provenience: Place or origin. In archaeological jargon this means the location (unit, test pit, soil layer, site etc.) in which the object was found.

Retouch: Evidence of re-sharpening along the working face of a stone tool.

ABOUT THE AUTHOR

Nick Adams has stumbled through a career in archaeology since first taking up a shovel as a sixteen year old in the UK. Working on various projects in Britain, he eventually ended up in Canada, at first working for the Province of Ontario in Sault Ste. Marie, then for a non-profit research foundation in Kingston, and later as a freelance archaeological consultant.

Unlike most who write books on archaeology, Nick has no pretensions to being a great academic or noted scientist. Nevertheless, he has successfully completed hundreds of archaeological assessment projects in Ontario, some of which were even a little bit interesting. After decades in the trenches, he finally got around to getting a piece of paper in 2003, earning an MA in Archaeology and Heritage (distinction) from the University of Leicester.

When he's not riding his 1970s Moto Guzzi motorbikes or hiking in the UK, Nick runs a small, active archaeological consulting company in eastern Ontario.

He has written two previous books (see over), a number of articles for 'RealClassic' motorcycle magazine, and is a regular contributor to many on-line forums.

Beyond the Coffee Shop: Riding 1970's Moto Guzzi Motorcycles in Northern Canada

"Canada is blessed with thousands of kilometres of empty roads which seem to wind on forever through forested hills and between still blue lakes. What better way to explore them than by riding 40 year old Italian motorbikes, famous for their dodgy electrics and sparse dealer network. 40 year old bikes, aged rider, thousands of kilometres of virtually unserviced empty roads in the middle of bear, wolf and blackfly infested wilderness - what could possibly go wrong?"

and......

Actually, I'm English: rediscovering my homeland on foot and by motorcycle

"Forty years is a long time to be away. Travelling on foot and by motorbike, Nick Adams discovers that while many things have changed, the things he loved; the hills, the pubs, the back roads and yes, even the weather, are undiminished. Join Nick as he hikes the length of Wales, hitting all the high spots. Then follow him up the spine of England on the Pennine Way, through brutal February weather. On his third trip, circumstances conspire against him. The original plan was to walk from Chepstow all the way to the Lake District. It didn't quite work out that way. Lastly, follow Nick across the North York Moors at night, then on across the country to the Cumbria coast. As if the snow, rain and endless miles weren't enough while hiking, jump on the back of the motorbike and ride from Scotland to Devon via Norfolk, dodging hypothermia, then through the Lakes, the Pennines and Wales. Nick's idea of a good time seems to involve bad weather, difficult terrain, stealth camping and innumerable pubs. This is one man's view of a country he loves, told in a simple, engaging style. Come along for the ride."

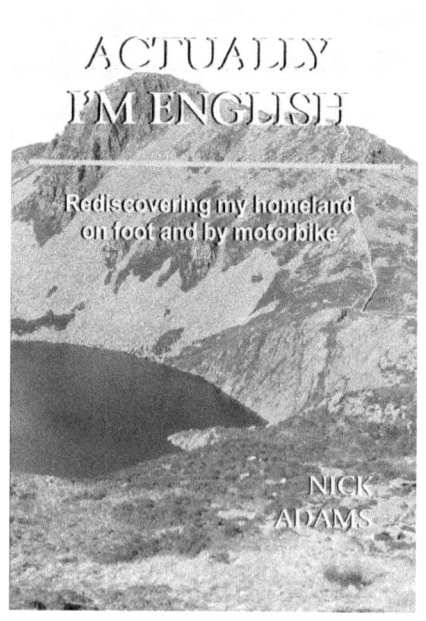

www.ingramcontent.com/pod-product-compliance
Lightning Source LLC
Chambersburg PA
CBHW072049280526
45788CB00006B/2236